RULES FOR PARENTS

RULES FOR
PARENTS

*Simple Strategies That
Help Little Kids Thrive—and You Survive*

Nan Silver

BERKLEY BOOKS, NEW YORK

This book is an original publication of The Berkley Publishing Group.

RULES FOR PARENTS

A Berkley Book / published by arrangement with
the author

PRINTING HISTORY
Berkley trade paperback edition / February 2000

The Penguin Putnam Inc. World Wide Web site address is
http://www.penguinputnam.com

ISBN: 0-425-16861-1

BERKLEY®
Berkley Books are published by The Berkley Publishing Group,
a division of Penguin Putnam Inc.,
375 Hudson Street, New York, New York 10014.
BERKLEY and the "B" design
are trademarks belonging to Penguin Putnam Inc.

PRINTED IN THE UNITED STATES OF AMERICA

10 9 8 7 6 5 4 3 2 1

The names in this book and some identifying details about the children have been changed, mostly to protect their clueless mother (usually, me).

For My Parents

ACKNOWLEDGMENTS

I am deeply grateful to the countless relatives, friends and colleagues whose wise advice is echoed in these pages. Heading this list, which would be too long to print in entirety, are my parents, Murray and Blanche, my sister Bonnie and my mother-in-law Flora. I would also like to thank the many experts I have interviewed in the course of my career whose research and wisdom made a lasting impression. Among them: Jay Belsky, Tiffany Field, Marilyn Gootman, John Gottman, Claire Kopp, William Pollack, Burton White, and Ed Zigler. Many thanks to my wonderful agent, Shelley Roth, for being a believer. Thanks also to Christine Zika. Thanks to Sonia Hylton. I could not have written this book without you.

Thanks to Diane, Dina, Jonine, June, Marcia, Mary, Sally and Susan—the girl's night octet. Thanks to the staff and parents of the Union Temple Pre-School—I learned so much from all of you. Thanks to the staff and parents of the Montclair Cooperative School, who are now furthering my education. Thanks for the great decaf, Ozzie's, Page One and Bluestone.

Thanks to my husband whose love, support, loyalty and willingness to put up with me and do without me made writing this book possible.

Finally, I thank my remarkable children who allow me to seem a far better mother than I am.

CONTENTS

Introduction

Where the Rules Came from and Why You Should Follow Them

I was eight months pregnant and in a panic. It had finally, fully sunk in that soon I would be a mother—and I had no idea how to take care of a baby. On paper I seemed well-qualified. I had been writing and editing magazine articles about child development for years. But now whenever I read baby-care advice, I froze. All of those manuals I thumbed through at the bookstore convinced me that taking care of a newborn was as complex and fraught with peril as safe-cracking or defusing bombs. How would I ever learn to breast-feed properly? Or diaper the baby? One book devoted an entire section to bathing, complete with what must have been some forty-five steps, including how to hold the baby, the correct positioning for wiping his eyes, even the precise order in which his body parts should be submerged in the tub. What if I did it all wrong? I wanted my baby to have the best care, but was I up to the job? My husband tried to comfort me: "Plenty of people dumber than us have become parents and their kids survived; ours probably will too." Feeling no better, I called my mother. She listened patiently as I despaired over the complex how-tos of baby shampoos. "What if I don't do it the right way?" I asked. "Darling," she replied, "the baby won't know the difference."

I had just learned my first Rule of parenting: You don't have to be perfect. Becoming a parent can feel so overwhelming, the new responsibility so heartfelt, that you can easily get sucked into trying to do things The Right Way and feel like a failure each time you botch it. And with young kids there are plenty of chances for botching. But little children are also very forgiving about screwups (as long as their safety isn't compromised) because they're completely ignorant. All they know of the world is what you present to them. Now whenever I feel like a flop because I caved when the tantrum reached ear-splitting proportions or I had to re-change a diaper after getting diaper-rash creme all over the adhesive tabs so they wouldn't stick, I remind myself of the Rule. It certainly takes the pressure off.

Since becoming a mother I've learned plenty of other rules that have made me a more successful parent. Not all of them are a direct inheritance from my mother. Thanks to my professional life as a magazine journalist and editor I've spoken with innumerable early childhood experts. Some, admittedly, weren't so expert. They seemed out of touch with what day-to-day life with a young child is really all about. But many were parents themselves who forged their perspectives in the trenches rather than just in the research lab. Valuable advice also came my way from my sister, mother-in-law, sister-in-law, cousins, friends and fellow beginning parents I met on park benches, playgrounds and pediatrician waiting rooms.

So here's the book that I wish I had found on the shelf amid all the how-to baby care manuals. Herein you'll find essential Rules for parenting infants, toddlers and preschoolers, culled and distilled from the good advice of countless parents, grandparents and researchers. Rules aren't about specifics. They don't resolve the timeless debates of parenting like whether babies should be burped on your shoulder or your lap, or whether pull-'em-up diapers help or hinder toilet training. Instead, these Rules are about the broader fundamentals. Taken together, they offer an approach, an *attitude* about raising little kids that just makes sense.

And what is that attitude? It's a mix of old and new ways of parenting that emphasizes love and respect, but not at the expense of firmness and discipline. It's not tough love, but it's not spineless either. Call it love with a backbone. Above all, it calls for making your child the central focus of your life. In these socially tumultuous and hypersensitive times, I'm not sure whether that makes the Rules revolutionary or reactionary, but this book is not about politics or social trends. It's about what's best for little kids. And what's best for them is to feel that there is at least one grownup in this world who puts them first. You don't put a child first by spoiling her, but by making decisions that will benefit her dramatically, whether or not those choices are most convenient for you.

Perhaps the best reason to master the Rules is that they will keep you from following other really bad ones. When you have a young child *everyone* is eager to give you advice, even if you don't want it—including the passerby who considers herself the ultimate authority on whether or not your baby should be wearing a hat. When you're new at the job, it can be hard to weed out the lousy advice from the good stuff, especially since wrongheaded strategies for taking care of babies and young children come from unexpected sources. I once interviewed an eminent obstetrician who proved to be not quite so expert on how to care for the babies she had delivered. We were walking together past her waiting room when a mother happened to lift her squalling six-week-old out of his carrier to comfort him. "Tsk, Tsk," said the doctor. "Don't pick him up, you're going to spoil him." The mother ignored this professional advice—and for good reason. You're *supposed* to spoil little babies. Responding to their seemingly endless need for comfort and caring is part of the job. It's how they develop a fundamental sense of security and stability, without which it's hard to grow up into a loving and confident human being.

I've found that bad rules for parents fall into two main categories, because there are two basic ways to screw up with little kids. The first is sort of the old-fashioned way. You so emphasize firmness and consistency that there isn't room left for sufficient love, joy and respect. The classic scenario is probably the wailing toddler at the supermarket whose longing to be picked up is responded to with a resounding whack on the rear end and a harsh "That'll teach you!" Once he's been reduced to whimpers his mother or father res-olutely ignores him. We've all heard the kind of rules that go along with this authoritarian approach: "Children should be seen and not heard," "Spare the rod, spoil the child." The old woman who lived in a shoe comes to mind.

The truth is, though, that some good-hearted parents still follow variations on this approach. Usually it's because they are unaware of the new findings on early childhood development. There was a time when most people didn't consider the treatment of young children all that important as long as it didn't involve cruelty. Early childhood was considered pretty inconsequential in the long run. Babies and toddlers were seen as sometimes adorable, sometimes incorrigible blobs who couldn't reason or remember much of anything. And if you're not going to remember, it doesn't really matter if your mother spanks you rather than gives you a time out. Or gives you bottles on a strict schedule even though you're ravenous between feedings.

But now we know that there are many different ways the brain remembers. You may not recall learning to walk, but your brain was developing at a remarkable pace while you were cruising around the living room sofa. Neurobiologists have gained tremendous insight into what happens inside a young child's brain. They can now document that connections between neurons—the brain's microscopic message and delivery system responsible for our ability to feel, learn and remember—are not completely hard-wired in at birth. Rather, many of these connections develop (or don't) beginning in early childhood, depending on your experience. You don't have to be a scientist to conclude that how children are treated during their first three years—how they're cared for and what they are exposed to—makes a monumental difference in the rest of their lives. The early years are a literal foundation for everything that lies ahead. Your personality, ability to learn, get along with others, develop language skills, all begins early on. If you want your children to be emotionally healthy and as happy, loving, and clever as they have the potential to be, you have to give them an enriching early childhood. And that means putting them at the center of your life and treating them with consideration.

Granted, most parents now recognize the importance of their child's first three years. But some who make great efforts in this area go about it in exactly the wrong way. They are following some modern rules which are just as destructive as the old-fashioned sort. One of the worst of these rules is to treat your child as if he were a little adult. This is supposed to show the child you respect him. I know one mother, for example, who refused to speak to her infant daughter in that high-pitched sing-songy voice so many parents adopt when talking to babies. She thought it was silly and condescending. After all, she'd never speak to a client that way, why should she subject her baby to it?

Well, some researchers have a name for that high-pitched, soothing speech—they call it "motherese" and they think they know why so many Moms seem to instinctively speak that way to infants. Turns out that a baby's brain is more responsive to high-pitched tones. Babies find such sounds stimulating, so they attune to them more than to other speech. Motherese therefore helps babies develop language and attachment to their mother. Certainly, no mom (or dad or baby-sitter) should feel she has to speak that way to a baby if it doesn't come naturally to her. There are lots of other approaches to bonding with an infant and stimulating her language capacity. But the point is that different standards of respect apply when dealing with a young child as opposed to an older one or an adult. You interact with young children in ways that would be ludicrous and insulting toward an adult, but are considerate of an infant's relative immaturity.

Then there are parents who become overly permissive with little kids, mistaking being lax for being respectful. This can be downright dangerous. When I was the still relatively ignorant mother of a two-month-old I listened intently while, between sips of decaf, the mother of a toddler pontificated to me on the right way to raise kids. Meanwhile, her two-year-old daughter was wandering unsupervised around the coffee bar, which was situated on a busy city street. "Aren't you worried that she'll run out into the traffic?" I asked. "Oh, no," said the mother. "She won't do that. She knows better because I've always given her plenty of independence. If you hover, children never learn to take care of themselves." "Don't Hover," sounded like a candidate for my fledgling list of Rules—at least for the thirty-odd seconds before her daughter bolted out the door. Fortunately a vigilant passerby saved her from an oncoming cab. After witnessing such episodes I did indeed add a new Rule to my list: "Hover." Teaching kids independence is a fine goal, but it's a *goal*, and certainly not one you should attempt to achieve while your child is still in diapers.

Another problem with permissiveness is that you can end up coddling your child to the exclusion of setting appropriate limits and teaching the rudiments of self-control—which is just a wordy way of saying that you risk turning him into a brat. Sure you want your child to know that you hear and understand him, but do you really want him to believe the universe is his playpen? At a street fair, I watched as a three-year-old deliberately doused a stranger's feet with his apple juice. His father bent down, put a hand on each shoulder and said, "Now Michael, I know how much fun it is for you to spill your juice like that. But I don't think that lady is happy now. Does she look happy?" Michael's dad then tried briefly to cajole an apology out of him, but Michael just ran away with a giggle. His father gave the woman an embarrassed shrug and followed after his son. "What that boy needs is a good spanking," said the victim as she watched father and son rush off. What he really needed was for his father to haul him back and clearly and firmly explain to him the rules of behavior. Then Dad should have insisted that Michael apologize to the woman he drenched. Michael would benefit a lot if his father would back-burner the "I hear you," approach in favor of some more "Now hear this!" Otherwise Michael is likely to end up with little regard for others.

Rules for Parents will help you avoid the pitfalls these parents fell into. It will prevent you from following approaches that are outmoded, dangerous or just plain dumb. In other words, it will allow you to learn from my mistakes.

If you attempt to follow a Rule and fail, take it from my mom: You don't have to be perfect. But it makes sense to keep striving. One thing that mitigates the stress of dealing with young children is that they are so impressionable. Which means you'll probably get plenty of chances to make the *right* impression.

Of course, no book can fully teach you how to be a parent, because raising kids just doesn't happen "by the book." Much of the time you find yourself improvising and bending the rules. That's okay. But it's not okay to liberally pick and choose from among these Rules, because then you may end up leaning too heavily toward being authoritarian or permissive.

Following the Rules doesn't guarantee that your children will grow up to be moral, happy, loving, generous, successful and grateful for all you did for them. But it increases the odds tremendously. And that's what parenting is really all about.

Chapter One

THE 25 GROUND RULES

1. You Don't Have to Be Perfect

Ever get that nagging feeling that you're bungling this whole parent thing—or are about to? Your instincts are right. The definition of parenting should include some mention of the fact that it is an impossible job. If you are the classic, obsessively worried parent it's time to let yourself off the hook.

As a parent you are almost inevitably compelled to maximize the chances that your darlings will grow up to be happy, kind and brave—not to mention brilliant, musically inclined, Olympic medalists. You are invested in their fortunes—from whether she gets invited to Rachel's birthday party to whether he's learning to read on schedule. And you fear that their failures will reflect your own flaws. Few parents subscribe to the bad seed theory in which rogue genes rather than a lousy childhood are held responsible when a kid goes wrong. If one day your beloved Richie blows up the playground or computer hacks his way into the Pentagon and upsets national security, you'll believe it's your fault. Even if your children don't grow up to be venal outlaws, but simply disappointments in areas of importance to you, you will still blame yourself. You will push rewind and carefully analyze every second of your interaction with said offspring to determine where you went wrong as a parent. All of this is a destructive and pathetic waste of time, but parents do it anyway.

To help you avoid this dead-end, here are two important secrets about being a parent. The first is that from the moment of birth you fail your child. You don't always know why he is crying. He turns to look at you but your face is turned away or he catches you wearing a frown. When he's a toddler he wanders away while you are sitting on a playground bench trading childbirth war stories with the other new moms. In the midst of someone's riveting account of her 150th hour of labor you suddenly hear, "Is this your child?" You look up to see your tearful two-year-old in the grip of a good Samaritan who found him wandering and crying out for you. As if that's not bad enough, when he goes to preschool you pick him up so late one day that his teacher has already left and he's been bequeathed to the office secretary who is teaching him how to merge files. In all of these instances he will look up at you with *J'accuse* written all over his face. And he has every right to be upset.

But the second secret is that what matters most is what happens next. Children don't just learn about you and the world when you do things right. They learn at least as much from studying what happens when you do things wrong. What's crucial then is to try to fix the situation. To pick up your crying baby. To hold your terrified toddler. To hug and apologize to your preschooler for being late. The experts have a word for this—they call it repairing. There are developmental psychologists who have spent day after day analyzing videotapes of mothers and babies. They've watched closely to see what happens when the baby is disappointed by Mom because, say, he smiles and she doesn't smile back or she walks away. In some way he lets his displeasure known. It's good news for the baby's future if the mom then smiles or coos or somehow tells the baby that everything is ok in their little world. She has repaired the situation.

Misconstruing or just missing each other's needs and then repairing the "miss" is the standard dance that occurs between all humans who love each other. It is a constant and endless process. This doesn't mean that all you have to say is "sorry" and you get to write off any horrible mistake you've made as a parent. You certainly can screw up your children by being a really awful parent. But you can't screw them up just by being imperfect.

So when you're holding your child in your arms feeling excruciatingly guilty because you forgot to pack her teddy for the trip to Grandma's, remember this: Thirty years hence she may well remember having to embark without her teddy bear, thanks to you. But now that she's grown up she can also thank you for her ability to feel love and to give it to her own mate and children—in her own imperfect way.

2. Don't Be Their Friend

With the world population hovering at six billion, there are plenty of people on earth who could be your child's playmate. You are not one of them. It is, perhaps, one of the necessary tragedies of parenthood that however much you like your kids you cannot be their pal, at least while they're young. Instead, you get to be the rain on their parade, the wet blanket at their party, the fly in their ointment. Not all the time, of course. But when a child needs guidance or correction someone has to do it. Out of those six billion, you're elected.

It's easier to cope with this unfortunate reality if you remember one of the cardinal truths about parenthood: It's a role. You can't just "be yourself" and succeed as a parent. Each of us has many different selves. There's the part of us that still thinks and feels like a child and would just as soon always be first, leave the crackers and cheese on the sofa, let someone else put away the Barbies, and stay up all night doing whatever wild, outrageous, and perhaps illegal things we used to do before we became parents. Then there's the responsible, sacrificing, reliable, nurturing part. It's clear which of your faces should be shining down on your kids. For children to grow up to be reasonable beings their parents have to act like, well, parents.

Fundamentally, the parent act entails making unpopular decisions. Unlike you, a good buddy would never enforce a regular bedtime, ban her from going to preschool wearing nothing but rain boots, or refuse to consider green gummy bears bonafide vegetables. This is what parents are for.

Of course, it's fine to be friendly with your kids. You can't be an effective parent if you're *not* playful much of the time. Children often learn better through play than through formal lessons. Whether you're teaching the ABCs or how to share, the message is more likely to sink in if your delivery is lighthearted.

But you still need to be the one who manages, organizes and, yes, controls their lives. Finding the balance between being playful and being a pal is an ongoing challenge. The best way to meet it is to be aware of your own motivations. Are you saying "yes" to the ice cream cone because now really is a good time for a treat or because you don't want to be a bad guy? If it's the latter you're better off saying "not today." No matter how heartily she protests, your child is lucky to have a parent who can stand up to her sweet tooth.

If you are able to strike this balance more often than not, you're likely to develop the kind of relationship that will greatly benefit your children when they reach adolescence. As teens there will certainly be things they will be reluctant to tell you. But if they respect and trust you there will also be things they will tell *only* you. This can be a vital safety net, so you don't want to wait until puberty to start weaving it. Your child's view of you—his understanding of your role in his life—starts now. So if your life with toddler resembles a buddy movie, consider toughening your act.

3. Say Yes Five Times More Than No

Couples who begin marriage counseling often discover that, whatever the therapy's effect on their marriage, it almost always makes them better parents. That's because certain principles—such as respect, empathy and effective communication—apply to all close relationships. If you were to distill the best marital advice into a single rule that would apply equally to parenting it would be: *Accentuate the positive.*

I know this thanks to Dr. John Gottman of the University of Washington. For more than twenty years he has been painstakingly researching why some marriages tick away happily while others go off like time bombs. Gottman has reams of videotapes which document volunteer couples talking together about everyday topics as well as arguing and making up. He uses a scientific method to code their verbal and body language second by second, along with every change in their heart rates, blood pressures and other physiological measures of tension and calmness. Based on this data he is able to predict whether each couple will eventually divorce or stay happily married. His accuracy rate is 91 percent.

Many factors figure into his predictions. But among the most salient is how often the couple is positive with each other as opposed to negative. Specifically, he finds that when couples are *five times more likely* to smile, talk pleasantly, and respond with interest to the other's comments than they are to be negative, their marriage is likely to flourish. On the other hand, if the negatives *outweigh* the positives, the relationship is pretty much toast. Gottman doesn't recommend eliminating the negative altogether (it has a place in a healthy marriage as well) but to overwhelm it with far more positive moments.

What works in marriage works with kids. If you raise your children with a 5:1 imbalance in favor of the positive your children are more likely to thrive. I don't think anyone has proven this by videotaping children, much less attaching a blood pressure cuff to their high chair. It's just common sense that the more positive you are with a child, the better everyone will get along. If your child feels you're fundamentally on her side, rather than on her case, she's going to feel good about herself—and about you. There's a huge payoff for her in the long run. And, for you—well, let's face it: A happy child is a lot easier to get along with and discipline than one who feels under siege.

If you build up plenty of good will, your child assumes you love and respect her. And that means that your three-year-old won't be overly traumatized when you do lose it now and then. Say it's Easter Sunday and you discover—as you're all heading out the door (late) to church—that Megan is no longer wearing her new dress and matching hat but her Tweety Bird pajamas and your bathing cap. Sure, in the best of times you might shower her with a delighted smile and tell her how wonderful she looks and how proud you are that she changed all by herself. Then, with great enthusiasm you'd race her back to her room and make a game out of seeing how fast she could change back.

But this is not the best of times, so most likely you will look at her aghast and say, "No, Megan! Absolutely not. You cannot wear your bathing cap to church." If the 5:1, positive: negative ratio has been operating in your home, there's a good chance, this being Easter and all, that she will say, miraculously, "OK Mommy" and let you help her change back quickly. If the 5:1 ratio is not in effect, however, it is pretty much preordained that she will start wailing, "But I want to wear a bathing cap!" leading you to pick her up off the floor and carry her back kicking and screaming into her room where you force her back into her tights and taffeta. It's quite possible, especially if she's been taking vocabulary lessons from an older sibling, that she will announce that she hates you forever.

One problem with a scene like this is that it can set the tone for an entire day. It's frighteningly easy to fall into a "No!" jag when dealing with little kids. The more you say "no," the more children may ricochet from one outrageous act to the next. So choose your battles wisely. Like spouses, little kids can only take so much nagging. But unlike spouses, few of them (yet) have the guts to face you squarely, hands on hips and say "lay off!" Instead, they fling their fork on the floor, or take off their diaper without telling you, or do any of a million annoying things that may seem like calculated attempts to drive you nuts but are really innocent signs that they are feeling overwhelmed and don't really know why. They just know things are not going the way they wished they would. So help them out. Keep a little 5:1 scale of kisses vs. hisses in your head. Make sure that on days when the "nos" seem to be ruling you dole out extra measures of hugs and laughter.

4. Talk about Feelings

Young children don't spend a lot of time pondering the deep mysteries like "Who am I?" or "What is the meaning of my life?" Existential angst doesn't usually erupt until acne does. Yet in their own way little ones are indeed trying to understand who they are.

The royal road to self-knowledge is to understand your emotions. Knowing that you're feeling angry, sad, happy or a mix of all these is the way you come to know yourself—what you care deeply about, what frightens you, pushes your buttons or delights you. The better you know yourself, the more rewarding and profound the relationships you'll be able to build with others.

People who have never been taught to understand their emotions may go through life without a clue as to what they are really feeling. Fired from a job or facing any other personal disaster they may just smile oh so sweetly or, instead, throw a thunderous tantrum at the express check-out lane when the person ahead of them is one banana over the limit. There are also people whose main identifying characteristic is a Vulcan-like emotionless, which is just as unappealing (except perhaps in airline pilots).

The way to prevent your children from growing up to be out of touch with themselves is to help them come to grips with what they are feeling from the time they are little. Although children are very emotional, being in tune with their feelings doesn't necessarily come naturally to them. Most can't verbally express the feeling behind their outburst or sudden impulse to throw a punch unless someone offers guidance. They need a calm, understanding adult to label the emotion for them. So when your child hits you it's best to say, "I can see you're angry." When he cries you say empathetically, "Oh, you're feeling sad."

Helping your child put words to her feelings in this way won't just help her understand her emotions, but eventually to control them when necessary. A child who is awash in an emotion may mistakenly experience the feeling as an extension of herself—as her identity. In other words, a two-year-old who is in a rage because she can't have another cookie is not necessarily aware that she is experiencing anger. Instead she *becomes* anger. Simply by giving her a word to explain what she is experiencing you make anger something that is separate from her, something that she can begin to control.

Your goal isn't just to help your child identify her feelings, but to guide her toward accepting them. One of the most important lessons you can teach a child is that having feelings—even nasty ones—doesn't make you "bad." When you let a child know that her negative or uncomfortable feelings are acceptable what you're really saying is that *she* is acceptable to you even when she's feeling furious, scared or sad. By getting this emotional *carte blanche* from an understanding parent a child comes to see herself as acceptable. This makes positive growth and change easier.

The more children learn to talk about their anger the less need they will have to act it out. They come to understand that there's a difference between feeling something—which is always okay—and *doing* something, which may not be. That's why nursery school teachers are always telling children "use your words" when they start to hit. If Susie squishes Russell's Play Doh pizza he's going to be outraged. If he can yell "That's mine. Don't do that. That makes me very angry!" he's less likely to hit her. No, you can't always curb a tantrum just by saying, "Hey Russell, tell her you're angry!" It takes a long time, and increased maturity, before children learn to always talk instead of act. But our job is to continually guide them along in this process.

Despite the clear good sense of this advice, it can be hard to follow if you're uncomfortable with your own feelings. If your parents were restrictive about expressing emotions you may feel overwhelmed by the primitive, raw nature of a little child's. Remind yourself that your child's intensity is normal and healthy for his age. Try to overcome your desire to curb it. If talking about feelings doesn't come naturally to you, get some storybooks on the subject to read to your child.

There are also parents who tend to deny or dismiss a child's negative emotions because they so desperately want to eradicate all painful experiences from their child's life. So, when Christina says "I'm scared," Mom says, "No you're not—there's nothing to be scared of." When she says, "I'm sad," Dad says, "Oh, no no, it's a happy day!" Though well-intentioned, this amounts to emotional brainwashing. It can leave a young child with the sense that what she's feeling is *not* what she's feeling—which hampers her self-understanding. Or she may come to believe that what she's feeling is not okay with Mom and Dad. This can make her feel like a big disappointment to them as well as lonely—it's as if nobody in the world understands her. She feels adrift in a sea of emotions with no one to help her cope. None of this is going to happen just because on occasion you say "don't cry," or "don't be scared." But a childhood full of this approach will rob children of the opportunity to really understand themselves.

4½. But Don't *Just* Talk about Feelings

Talking about emotions is important, but it's not the trump card of parenting. In many situations, helping your child identify what he's feeling is only step one in a process that ends with him not only understanding himself but also where his rights end and other people's begin. If you raise your child to be sensitive and aware of feelings he's more likely to grow up to have a rich and fulfilling life. But if you raise him to be sensitive and aware only of *his* feelings, all he'll grow up to be is a brat.

Watch as Matilda's mom takes one small step in that unfortunate direction. Matilda, age three, is in the midst of a tea party with her dollies when Mom interrupts to announce it's bath time. Matilda responds by flinging a tiny porcelain creamer through the air. Because she is at the age where many children begin to make the transition from expressing their anger physically to offering up verbal abuse, she also lets loose with, "I don't like you Mommy. You go die forever!"

"You're very angry," Mom tells Matilda. (*Good labeling of her daughter's emotions.*)

"Yes!" says Matilda. "I'm playing. Don't bug me!"

"You wish I would leave you alone," says mother. (*More fine labeling.*)

"Yes, go away!"

"Well I came to tell you it was time for your bath, but if you're still playing you can wait a while longer." (*Uh-oh.*)

Mom breaks two important rules. The first is never to give a porcelain tea set to a three-year-old. The second is never to let your child get away with outrageous behavior. Mom did a great job of labeling Matilda's feelings. But she was so acutely focused on teaching little Matilda emotional self-knowledge that she also taught her that Mommy is a doormat.

You want your child to understand and accept her own feelings. But you also want her to respect other people, starting with you. So whenever your child calls you names, hits, bites, or otherwise expresses anger in the uncivilized ways that befit her age you should respond with this four-point plan.

1. **Identify and validate the feeling:** As per Rule #5 say, "You're feeling very angry that it's time to clean up. That's why you are biting me/calling me names/hurling breakables or edibles in my direction."

2. **Lay down the law:** Address the behavior and connect it to consequences. "But it hurts my feelings when you call me names. In this family we don't talk to each other that way. I don't want you to do that anymore." "It's okay to feel angry, but it is not okay to throw your toys. Now Mommy has to put the tea set away for the rest of the day. You can try again tomorrow to play with it the right way."

3. **Stick to your guns:** Since step 2 may provoke a tantrum you may be tempted to back off . But if you give in you'll be rewarding her for the words and actions you're trying to eradicate. Instead, say, "Angry or not, it's still time for your bath."

4. **Move on:** Don't dignify behavior you don't like by spending a lot of time discussing it. Sometimes kids misbehave in order to get

your attention. So if you heap it on they'll keep acting out to get more and more. No matter how shockingly, outrageously colorful your child's behavior or language, be direct, quick and to the point in your response. And then get back to folding the laundry.

5. Teach Them to Enjoy Life

"It is fun to have fun,

But you have to know how."

—The Cat in the Hat

Aimee has very definite ideas about childrearing. She thinks if you give children only healthy food they'll learn to prefer oatmeal to Oreos. She believes that it's a parent's responsibility to keep them away from treats that are nutritionally worthless, ultra-processed and full of chemicals; treats that will someday be linked to everything from mad cow disease to male-pattern baldness. She thinks you should never let them watch any TV other than PBS and that all their toys should be educational. If my friend Aimee sounds like the perfect mother, it's because she's not a mother at all. Before I had kids of my own I agreed with Aimee. I still do. But I'm grateful for my children's sake that I don't raise them completely the way I "should."

In these days of bike helmets for trike riders, car seats, sunblock and infant CPR classes, it's easy to overlook that a parent's role is not just to keep kids safe—it's also to teach them to enjoy life. This doesn't mean you let them jump in the pool without a floater, or eat raisins before they even have teeth. It does mean, though, that on occasion you let them eat Malomars, watch some mindless TV shows, jump on their beds, stay up late to watch fireworks, and buy them disgusting, educationally worthless toys like plastic vomit. Childhood should be lived in Technicolor—it's a vibrant, exciting, giddy time. At least it should be. Kids don't need the hottest new toy to have fun. But they do need to get a message from their parents that it's all right to be a kid.

My son's first pediatrician told me sternly that "chocolate is not for young children, it's an adult food." Every time I look at the photos of his first birthday party, his face coated with the chocolate icing from his cake and a look of otherworldly bliss in his eyes, I'm glad that banning chocolate is one bit of advice I didn't add to my list of Rules.

6. Get Help in a Hurry

Most pediatricians do not appreciate being awakened at five A.M. every time a child falls out of a crib. But what if it's *your* child who's taken the plunge? Now that her tears are dried she's fallen back into a deep sleep. The baby-care book says this could be a sign of a concussion. Of course, it could also be a sign that she wasn't badly hurt and therefore went back to sleep. Should you rouse her and hot-tail it to the ER? Or should you call your pediatrician? Call. He may wish you hadn't, but this is part of his job. He'll probably ask you a few questions to assess the situation and then tell you not to worry. Now, you'll be able to get some sleep.

You probably have friends who wouldn't dream of calling the pediatrician unless their child turned blue. They let their baby crawl around their 1901 vintage colonial home without having it tested for lead paint dust and leave their two-year-old alone in the tub with nothing but a rubber ducky while they cook dinner. And you probably know someone who worries more— like the friend who insists her baby-sitter write down every ounce of food her child eats and demands documentation of the day care center's supposedly low radon readings.

The typical new parent falls somewhere between these extremes—but many of us skew toward the more nervous end of the spectrum. Which means that while you may not qualify as obsessive, you will probably be anxious. Worrying is part of the job description when you become a new parent. Those with more experience used to counsel me to "just relax." This would have been reasonable advice if it weren't impossible to follow. I couldn't relax simply because I decided to. I relaxed when my anxieties were alleviated. And that occurred only when I did whatever it took to ease my mind. Sometimes that meant inconveniencing somebody else, like calling the pediatrician at off hours because the soft spot on my daughter's head seemed to be pulsing too much or too little or I couldn't find it altogether.

Almost always this sort of catastrophic worry turns out to be unwarranted. When my son was about a year old he developed what seemed to be a tremor—suddenly his fists would clench and his entire body would start shaking. After witnessing this a handful of times my husband and I were convinced something was dreadfully wrong. One night, as my son sat in his high chair we stood in front of him discussing the problem. We had decided that I would call the pediatrician first thing in the morning. "Yes," I said to my husband, "But I'm not sure what to say the problem is—a tremor? A convulsion? How do you describe . . ." and I started shaking in imitation of my son. Right on cue my son started shaking, too, and then squealed with delight. Instead of suffering from some rare neurological disorder he had simply been performing his first "stupid human" trick.

Now it's a funny story, but at the time we had been terrified. So don't chide yourself or your spouse for being an alarmist. Better to know that the headache isn't meningitis and the cough isn't pneumonia than to not call the doctor because you're embarrassed or afraid.

At the top of the parental worry-wart list are not just clear-cut medical concerns like what to do when the thermometer reads 106, but developmental ones—like what to do when a two-year-old isn't talking yet or a four-year-old doesn't want to play with other children.

Most parenting books tend to be very encouraging when it comes to development—emphasizing that there's a range of what's normal and therefore no need for concern if a child hits milestones at the far end of the range—like not rolling over until six months and not walking until seventeen months. Usually, this is so. But there's no guarantee that it's true for your child. **DON'T WAIT**. If your child seems to be lagging behind his peers, or you just have a gut instinct that something seems "off," seek professional advice immediately.

Thirty years ago if you were concerned about your two-year-old's speech you'd probably be reassured that he'd start talking eventually and that two was too young to intervene anyway. There was no urgency to seeking help since there wasn't much help you could get. But now that it's well known how crucial these early years are for a child's future, and there are therapies available to help with all sorts of delays, it just makes sense to be alert for warning signs (even if they are only in your own mind) and get your child evaluated as early as possible.

Having your child checked out can go a long way toward alleviating your fears. If a thorough evaluation of the "problem" determines that there isn't one, let it go. If you can't, consider that your worry may have more to do with your own personal issues than what's going on with Andrew's sleeping or Sarah's speech development.

At the same time, be cautious before presuming that experts are always right when they do find a problem. There is a tendency nowadays to pathologize normal variations in development because our culture insists kids grow up so fast. For example, five-year-old Max's parents were advised by his preschool teacher that he needed occupational therapy because his hand muscles weren't yet strong enough to write legibly. His parents made the round of specialists and got a wide spectrum of opinion concerning the need to intervene. But every expert confirmed that there was nothing wrong with Max's hands—they just needed more time to develop muscle strength. So his parents thanked the teacher for her advice—and then wisely ignored it. By the time he entered kindergarten Max was able to write his name. His handwriting was still awkward but not awful enough to burden him with therapy. Instead his parents worked with his kindergarten teacher to make the classroom a happy place for him and his hands "as is." The moral here, of course, is not to mindlessly follow some expert's advice.

That said, keep in mind that the absolutely worst thing you can do if anyone raises concerns about your child is to *ignore* it. Denial is an understandable reaction to anxiety, but shutting your ears to painful or unwelcome news usually just makes matters worse. Take the cases of Rueben and Oliver, three-year-old boys in the same nursery school class. At parent-teacher conferences in the late fall the teacher tells both sets of parents that their child seems to have a developmental delay and recommends he be evaluated. Rueben's mother, though skeptical, decides that just in case the teacher has picked up on something she'll have him evaluated by a learning specialist right away. Within two weeks she gets the word that her son does indeed have a language delay and early indications of an attention disorder. Through the city's board of education Rueben's parents get him the necessary therapy. By age five, Rueben has caught up enough with other children to attend a regular kindergarten.

But Oliver's parents brush off what the teacher tells them. Sure, Oliver has been slow to talk and a bit shy, but his grandparents say his uncle was the same way at three and grew out of it. When the nursery school tells them that Oliver should not return the following year because the school is not a suitable setting for him, they don't get the message, they just get mad. The school doesn't understand their child, the teachers are alarmists. Instead of having their child tested they move him to a different preschool. Eventually, the new school raises concerns, since Oliver is now behaving aggressively toward other children. Finally Oliver's parents have him evaluated. The results are similar to Rueben's, but they come a year and a half later. Oliver is slated for a special education class.

It's understandable to feel anger, resentment and disbelief when a professional raises concerns about your child. Ultimately, the decision about what to do (or not do) about your child's situation is yours. But the more information you have, the better able you'll be to choose a course of action. When in doubt, always get it checked out.

7. Sometimes Nothing Works

Newborns don't do much other than sleep, cry, drink, and poop. Sounds simple at first. But then, so do some of life's most complex problems. Soon after my friend Gina brought her newborn son home from the hospital she was stymied by the following: whether to change his diaper before or after breast-feeding him. Her goal, of course, was for him to nurse and then drift off into blissful sleep like all the babies in the nursing videotapes they showed her at the hospital. But inevitably, her son would poop right before or during his feeding. If she changed his diaper first, by the time she brought him to her breast he would be sucking and crying at the same time because he was so hungry. This would lead to spit up and gas, which prevented him from sleeping. She tried changing him after a feeding but this would wake him up, which would start the whole scream/suckle/spit-up/poop cycle all over again. She even tried letting him drain one breast and then changing him before giving him the second one. But putting him on the changing table also made him spit up, which got him so upset that the one remaining breast wasn't enough to soothe him to sleep.

"What should I do?" she asked me.

So I told her the truth. "There's nothing you *can* do." And then I added, "Get used to it."

That's just how it is with all children, not just newborns. Sometimes *nothing* works and you're left to muddle through. Almost always, kids outgrow whatever insurmountable problem they have presented to you. In the meantime, you just try to outlive it. In the morning you change the diaper before the nursing. If that doesn't work you try changing it halfway through at the next feeding. On some days you get lucky, on others you get frustrated. Meanwhile, the baby keeps growing until he's out of the spit-up and yellow poop stage and ready to present you with even more ghastly problems.

Part of being a parent is to try really, really hard to solve these problems. But part of being a parent is also to realize when you can't. When, instead, you just have to make do, attempting to keep your sense of humor intact.

Some kids, for example, are nearly impossible to potty train. They are certainly "ready" according to every checklist you've ever seen. But they just don't want to. The months go by. The child is two, two and a half, three, three and a half. You've been changing diapers for so long that the fragrant scent of a clean wipie has come to smell like poop to you. You read, you consult, you cajole, you bribe. You leave the kid alone. You buy a different potty. You buy a videotape, a book, a doll, spaceman underpants. Nothing works. Then one day your child just starts using the toilet. He will, of course, choose the day that you're traveling back from visiting Grandma in Cleveland, so that you have to take him to the bathroom on the plane and in both airports. But it's worth it. You didn't solve the problem, you survived until it solved itself.

This rule holds especially when it comes to discipline. There is no magic punishment or script that will get kids to treat you, themselves, other people and property the way they should. As soon as you allow the toy pirate ship to come back down from the top shelf, they start fighting over it again. Her time-out is all done and she proceeds to kick you. What can you do? Try disciplining her again, but inwardly accept the limitations of your control.

It's certainly dangerous to consider any of your child's worrisome behavior simply a stage that he or she will "get over." I'm not suggesting you shrug these problems off. The bad news is that both things are true. If something isn't going well for your child, you may not be able to fix it, or even *need* to fix it—but you still have to devote enormous amounts of energy to trying.

Then, at some point, you need to get philosophical about your helplessness if nothing works. All you can do is pray that thanks to the massive accumulation of your attempts, by the time he's thirty he will be lovable even to those who didn't know him back when spit-up interfered with his sleep.

8. Be Patient

It's a typical morning. You need to drop off your child at daycare/your mother's/preschool/the baby-sitter's before heading for work. You're five minutes late so, of course, your child:

A) Is eating his Cheerios one "O" at a time.

B) Will not let you dress her until she shows you every item she wants from some toy catalogue.

C) Insists on zipping his own jacket—a laborious process at the best of times. If you try to help he will take it off and start over.

D) Just decided to expand her fear of bees and wasps to include every benign creepy crawler known to humanity. She will not leave the house without first surveying the front lawn. You convince her that what she sees on the path is not an ant but a black speck. "What's a thpeck?" she asks suspiciously. Before you can answer, a bonafide ladybug crawls across the slate. She screams and dashes back into the house.

E) Gobbles his English muffin and rushes off to brush his teeth all by himself. In two minutes flat he declares, "All ready."

F) All of the above except E.

If you checked E you can skip this rule. For everyone else, here's a crash course in patience.

For starters, understand where impatience with little kids comes from. When you become a parent the control you have over your day decreases in direct proportion to your expanding joy. What used to be a ten-minute run to the supermarket is now an hour expedition, what with dressing baby, bringing diapers, wipes, searching for that rattle and taming the tantrum that occurs after you block your two-year-old's attempt to knock over all of the pickle jars.

Becoming a parent adds meaning and pleasure to your life. But it also means that for the foreseeable future you *have* no life. You cannot bathe two children, make dinner, read stories and get everyone to bed by 8:00 if you take a moment to clip your toenails. Until you fully accept this you will be impatient with your children, waiting for things to get back to normal which, of course, will never happen.

Your sinking sense that your life is essentially over will be readily confirmed by the world out there, which remains oblivious to the needs of small children and their parents. Most bosses do not consider "My daughter pooped in the potty for the first time," a valid excuse for punching in late. The working world is unforgiving when your schedule gets screwed up by a two-year-old's tantrum or your baby-sitter's personal problems which preclude her from giving you fair warning (or at least five minutes warning) that she has to visit her sick uncle and therefore will not make it to work today or any day for the next ten years. So, while you are watching your child fumble stubbornly with his zipper you are tallying the consequences—ranging from an irate, finally-fed-up boss, to another late night making up for the work you're not doing now. Either way, you're not likely to get enough sleep tonight, which means that by tomorrow morning your patience will be missing altogether. No wonder you're ready to pull up that zipper yourself. A patient parent is the oxymoron of the 00s.

It helps to remember that your kids aren't driving you crazy deliberately. They have no concept of how long it takes to do something, or think something. The amount of time they spend watching an ant crawl across the path could be five seconds or five hours. Because their concept of time is so flexible they don't understand why you are so uptight about it.

It would be unrealistic and probably even harmful if you never expressed impatience toward your children. Having to cope with your frustration when they dawdle helps them learn there can be fallout when they are uncooperative. You don't want them to assume that they can inconvenience you enormously, even put your job at jeopardy, and still be treated like little angels. But there is a difference between losing your cool on occasion and at twenty-four-hour intervals.

As frustrating as it is to deal with a dawdling child when you are late, there are many downsides to acting impatient on a regular basis. (*Being* impatient you might not be able to avoid. But acting impatient is a tendency you can unlearn). For one thing, it's rude. When you say "hurry up, hurry up" in increasing decibels they feel about you the way you do about a tailgater. Being impatient with little children is also not a way to maximize their developmental potential. It does not create a warm, unthreatening environment in which they can explore, expand their minds and grow into the kind of (prompt) people you want them to be.

But perhaps the most practical (if not the most important) reason for curbing your impatience with little children is that rushing them is almost certain to backfire. If, instead of punctuating his attempts to zip with "Come on, hurry up, here let me do it!" you offer up some slow, encouraging words like "You can do it. Try again. There you go," the time expenditure will be less in the long run. Taking the extra minute helps avoid a scene. Once the tears and kicking start you have a miserable child to contend with, as well as more delays—especially if you need to put him or her in a time out and talk out what just happened.

You probably already know more than you care to about the perils of impatience. So why do you fall prey to it while other parents don't? What is the secret of that perfectly coifed mom who drops off her child at day care meticulously dressed, no toast crumbs at the corners of her mouth, and matching bows in her hair? Why is this mother always smiling in the elevator while you are gritting your teeth? Either she is a sociopath, heavily medicated, or has had the foresight to strictly adhere to the following advice:

Schedule in dawdling time.

This is the reverse of that old rule about preparing for a trip: Pack everything you think you absolutely need, and then put half of it back. With little kids you need to schedule in as much time as you can possibly imagine needing to get somewhere—and then double it. This way there is time to let them zip their jackets or peruse toy catalogues, or to say "no" to these requests for good reasons—not because you don't have time to discuss them intelligibly. It means you will have time for a long talk about what makes bugs scary, and maybe even some deconditioning. With luck, this means that tomorrow morning she will venture boldly onto the front path. If, instead, you must carry her screaming to the car because the clock is ticking, you will pay the next morning—which may mean you'll be even later.

Talk yourself down.

Yes, it really helps to take a deep breath, label your feelings, a la "I'm getting impatient," and force yourself to cool it. You do this by first focusing on how your body is reacting to your impatience. Probably your jaw is clenched, along with almost every other muscle in your body. By purposefully relaxing those muscles you halt the feedback loop that unwittingly adds to your stress (you're upset, your pulse rate quickens, which makes you feel more upset, which ups your pulse all the more, etc.). Next, pretend you're being filmed. The *60 Minutes* cameras are rolling, documenting a day in the life of the typical toddler. There he is, putting Cheerio number thirty-seven into his mouth. Now let's get Mom's reaction. Close-up. Smile for the camera, Mom. It's easy to let loose your patience in the privacy of your own home—but not if you imagine the whole world is watching.

Be clear about your rules.

If you have to say "Five more minutes" four times before your children hup to, what you're really saying is "twenty more minutes." By minute nineteen you probably feel like you're about to combust. But it's not really impatience you're feeling—it's anger at yourself for letting your kids rule the house. That anger gets bottled up and then unleashed on your child. So don't say "five more minutes" unless you mean it and if you mean it let them know, even if that means physically removing them from the premises when the time is up.

Admit it.

Let your kids know you're getting impatient. Apologize. Tell them you'll try harder next time. You may not be the most patient parent, but at least you're giving them the message that you don't consider yourself perfect, which means it's okay for them to make mistakes too.

Of course, not all of the impatience we feel with young children is due to time pressure. In some cases our impatience comes from concerns about the child's maturity—or lack thereof. By our measure he should be out of diapers already, or speaking in full sentences, or able to write his name. After all, his sister could at his age, and so can most of the kids in his nursery school class. Perhaps he is intentionally dragging his feet. Often, this kind of impatience is really a screen for parental anxiety when a child seems on the late side in passing some milestone. Instead of admitting our concern to ourselves we blame the child. In all such cases, expressing impatience doesn't help and is almost always harmful. It's far better to admit to yourself that you're worried. That way you can deal with the issue objectively and see more clearly whether it is unfounded or reality-based. The solution could be anything from having your child professionally evaluated to backing off and letting her decide when and where to pee. There are many "right" paths in these situations. But impatience with your child is a certain dead end.

9. Teach Them to Make Choices

Start when they are toddlers. Instead of "put on your pants," try, "would you like to wear your red pants or blue ones?" Instead of "time to go," say, "should we put on your hat first or your mittens?" Giving them a choice in the matter lets them feel more in control of their day—thus helping *your* day go more smoothly. It's a great strategy for preventing tantrums: Your toddler gets distracted enough choosing the color of his pants that he forgets to get balky over having to get dressed to go out when he'd rather stay home and watch Big Bird.

But offering a choice is more than a ploy. It also begins your child on the long journey toward becoming his own person. It's easy to argue that who you are and what you accomplish in life is rooted in the decisions you make. It takes practice to get it right. Children who are raised by authoritarians who make their decisions for them, often flounder in early adulthood when they have to fly solo. Since Mom always woke her up so she'd get to school on time, she's never had to decide for herself the pros and cons of being on time versus sleeping till noon. She's been disciplined, no doubt, but she hasn't learned *self*-discipline. Kids raised in this kind of household may grow up to be ultra-rigid, doing everything exactly the way Mom and Dad taught them, even if circumstances suggest it's time for a change. Or, they may grow up to feel lost and ineffectual because they haven't had the opportunity to develop the problem-solving tools adulthood requires.

It's almost unfathomable now, but eventually your child will be making decisions about what to wear, whom to befriend, which job to pursue. The best way to help him make the best choices down the road is not to choose everything for him now. Whenever you can, give him the opportunity to decide what he eats, wears, plays with. By preschool age you can also ask leading questions to help guide him toward making wise decisions. If it's raining out don't immediately reach for his rain coat. You can point to the rain through the window and ask him how his body might feel if he wears just his sweater. Ask, "Which coat do you think you should wear today?" Say "good thinking!" when he concludes for himself that his slicker is the best choice.

As with all aspects of parenting, overdoing this rule can be disastrous. Allowing your child to wear only his sweatshirt during a blizzard isn't teaching him to take responsibility for his choices, it's being irresponsible as a parent. For years to come, your child is going to need plenty of guidance—you will have to assert plenty of control. One of the most important ways you do this is by limiting his choices to options you find acceptable. At the dinner table he can choose his own vegetables—carrots or string beans. But you also make it clear that the marshmallows in the pantry are *not* on the menu.

10. Be Their Squeaky Wheel

Someday your child will be wronged. The pediatrician will mistakenly pooh pooh a serious symptom, a teacher won't notice she never raises her hand, no one intervenes when a bully keeps terrorizing him. Sometimes you'll witness these troubles yourself, other times your child will come to you with them. In all such cases your role isn't just to comfort your child but to problem-solve.

On occasion this entails helping your child change his or her behavior or take a different view of what's happening in class or on the playground. You want your child to learn to assert himself, to stand up for his needs and rights, to learn that the squeaky wheel is the one that gets the oil. But often, especially when kids are so young, they have a hard time being their own advocate—they need you to do it for them. No matter how assertive they are, little kids may not squeak loud enough for grownups in positions of power over them to take notice. So speak up on their behalf.

Most of us do watch out for our children in this way. The problem is that sometimes our style of going about it defeats the purpose. The tricky part about being an advocate is that to be effective you often have to leave your emotions out of it. Yet most people feel highly emotional when they think their child has been mistreated or misjudged. That protective instinct comes out in full battle gear. Even before you have all the facts, you go ballistic.

That's what almost happened when Sondra had a parent-teacher conference at her son's nursery school. The teacher had high praise for Tom, an extremely bright and well-behaved boy. "There's just one thing that bothers me," the teacher added with a sigh of frustration. "No matter how often I tell him, he just refuses to color within the lines when we do art projects." As a case in point, she showed Sondra a pile of paper pumpkins she had outlined for the children to color for Halloween. Most of the pumpkins were indeed neatly tinted with orange crayons. But Tom's page was a profusion of joyous, multi-colored scribbles. As the teacher clucked her tongue Sondra felt her fury and anxiety grow.

For starters, Sondra thought it was ridiculous—and even potentially damaging—to insist a three-year-old color within the lines. And she knew she had countless early childhood experts on her side. There is a reason many preschools have banned coloring books. Many now believe that it's more productive to let a child's imagination—and his crayons—roam all over the paper than to insist on proper technique. The point shouldn't be the finished product, but the process. Children should feel the pleasure and power of creating their own picture, and feel respected for it. This do-your-own-thing approach to art in early childhood used to be considered progressive but has become commonplace enough that the label may no longer fit.

Paul's teacher seemed so behind the times to Sondra that her first instinct when she saw that pile of perfect pumpkins was to pull him out of the school. But she did a quick mental assessment and concluded that this would harm Paul more. Sondra was a single mother who lived in a neighborhood where there weren't many children her son's age. At first he had been very shy at school and uncertain about playing with his classmates. Now he was in his full glory. Everyday he'd come home and announce what "me and my friends" did.

So Sondra just took a deep breath, pointed to Paul's pumpkin and said to the teacher, "I understand this bothers you, but it isn't a big deal, is it?" The teacher assured her it was not. Sondra plainly and politely asked the teacher to leave Paul alone about it. "He loves school so much. I don't want anything to interfere with his happiness about being here." The teacher agreed. End of story—with a postscript. About a month later Sondra photocopied an article on this newer approach to preschool art for Tom's teacher. It didn't change his teacher's mind completely but she thanked Sondra for the article and said it gave her much to think about.

When it comes to advocating for their kids most parents fall into one of three categories. Some are too meek. These are the parents who are intimidated by teachers, pediatricians, and other adults who have professional knowledge of their children and fear offending them by challenging their decisions. The problem with this approach is obvious—these parents don't really advocate for their children. They need to remember that they know their child better than any professional and that these days, taking care of a youngster's needs in many areas has to be a partnership between parents and the expert. Assertiveness training is called for if you're not up to this task.

The second group is made up of moaners and groaners who never think other people do enough, care enough or are good enough for their child. And although these parents get their way at times, they do it by bullying. An attitude of disrespect can backfire. One preschool teacher, for example, never told a bullyish Mom that she suspected her son needed speech therapy. She considered the child to be a borderline case. In most such circumstances she would mention casually to the parent that it might be a good idea to have the child assessed. But she knew if she mentioned it to this mother she would be deluged with tirade after tirade for criticizing her son. So she said nothing. The next year, in kindergarten, the child's parents were finally told he needed therapy. His preschool teacher was wrong for not alerting this mother to her concerns. But teachers are human. So when dealing with your child's it pays to treat them as such.

The third group of parents are effective advocates. Why? Because they tend to do the following:

Ask questions.

Often problems are the result of a misunderstanding. If you think your child has been placed in the wrong nursery school class there may be a myriad of reasons. The school may perceive his maturity level differently than you do, they may have made a mistake, you may be mistaken about the class's makeup, etc. So begin your advocacy by gathering information. That means instead of saying, "This is unacceptable. I want my son's class changed. Most of the children in his class are barely three and he's almost four. I insist he be moved," you say, "Can you explain to me how you made the decisions for class placements? It seems to me that most of the other children in my son's class are younger than him and I'm wondering why that is."

Make suggestions, not demands.

No matter how deep your concern, you're likely to be more effective if you don't bark orders. Instead of, "I *insist* you test Tina for strep throat!" say "I know you don't think Tina has strep throat, but it's been going around her daycare center and she hasn't wanted to eat much. Would you mind taking a throat culture just to rule it out? This is very important to me."

Appeal to a higher authority.

If the problem still has not been satisfactorily resolved in your mind, don't give up. Keep pushing for your child. Often that means going to the school's director or the head of the clinic. Stay calm, outline the problem as you see it, offer your suggestions again.

Yell like hell.

Sometimes you have to. In the end it's more important to protect your child than to be polite. But by following the advice above it's unlikely you'll have to resort to this tactic.

Advocating for your child has benefits even if you lose. You show your child that you love and respect her enough to put yourself out there. Plus, you've demonstrated for her how to be assertive. This dramatically increases the chances that she will get what she wants in life—except, of course, when dealing with an airline.

11. Teach the Magic Words

You may be tickled to bits the first time your formerly docile tot masters "Gimme dat!" But the charm of a child who's more Goofus than Gallant won't last. Manners matter.

Training your kids to offer up "pleases" and "thank yous" in social circumstances is one of the best gifts you can give them. Sure, in our fast-paced society teaching manners is going the way of perfect penmanship. But you don't have to be a charm-school graduate to know that polite people are better liked and more successful than rude ones. And if fewer people are raised to be well-mannered, teaching your kids to be polite will just make them shine all the more.

Early childhood is absolutely the easiest time to teach manners, since etiquette is one of those areas of parenting that calls for out-and-out brainwashing. Your kids will never again be as impressionable as they are now. What you want is to make certain responses automatic. For help, check out your local library or a bookstore. Their shelves are rife with propaganda tracts on the joys of good manners, cleverly disguised as engaging toddler books featuring Bert and Ernie and just about every other PBS morning programming star. Kids learn from example. It's frightening how readily they'll take suggestions from a huge fuchsia dinosaur or a toothless puppet who's been wearing the same striped shirt for about thirty years.

Bolster the message these storybooks deliver by reminding your child what to say as circumstances arise. You don't have to demand etiquette every time your child gets demanding. You just have to remind him of what he's *supposed* to do. "What's the magic word? Say please! Say thank you! Say excuse me!" If he doesn't give the right answer—or any answer—don't scold. Instead, just supply it yourself. Eventually he'll catch on.

Of course, a well-mannered two-year-old won't necessarily stay that way at twelve. At that age your kids may turn into hormones with feet and develop amnesia for all forms of civilized behavior. But the early childhood training is likely to resurface years later, just in time for facing job interviews and the opposite sex. So start now. If your baby can say "Mama" she's ready to practice "Peez."

12. Respect Their Fears

"There's nothing to be afraid of."

"Look at all the other children. Do they look scared? No! They're having fun."

"Charlie, you're being silly."

Four-year-old Charlie's dad thought there was only one problem—his son was afraid of the water. He had signed him up for spring swimming lessons at the Y because they were planning to spend much of the summer poolside. But on the first day of class, while the other kids all happily shimmied into the pool, Charlie wouldn't even let the teacher put on his floatie. He stared at the water in horror, as if it were home to some sea monster visible to his eyes only. He clung to his father. His dad was right—this was a big problem. But it wasn't as big as Charlie's second problem, which was his dad. Frustrated, angry and embarrassed (why was *his* kid the fraidy cat?) Charlie's dad had a hard time sympathizing with his son. Week after week this went on. His dad tried coaxing, begging, bribing, scolding, shaming. He made Charlie sit there and watch all the other kids learn to swim. It didn't work.

Hey, maybe nothing would. Plenty of kids aren't ready to take the plunge into a pool at four. But Charlie didn't just have his age against him—he also had a parent who didn't respect his fear of the water. So instead of just feeling scared, he felt scared and alone. Nobody seemed to understand him. His father was angry with him. He was trying to help Charlie get rid of his fear. But instead he was just forging a connection in Charlie's mind between being afraid and feeling humiliated and embarrassed.

The solution to this problem was probably obvious to everyone in the world who wasn't in the middle of it—stop the swimming lessons! So you wasted some money. So Charlie will spend the summer digging for worms while his buddies dog paddle away. So what? It's all a small price to pay for letting your child decide for himself when he's ready to conquer his fear.

Respecting a child's fears certainly doesn't mean that you accept them as "legitimate." The cow mooing on the TV screen cannot harm your terrified tot. The leashed dog down the street poses little threat. The Cavity Goon cannot jump out of the Timmy the Tooth videotape and make nocturnal visits to your four-year-old's bedside, no matter what he believes. But it does mean that you don't say "there's nothing to be afraid of," because obviously there is—the child is afraid of his imagination and that's tough to tame in early childhood. So you might as well acknowledge the bogeyman as existing—in your child's head. The worst approach is to laugh at a frightened child. It may seem funny when a tot cries every time he sees a clown's face, but it's not at all funny to him.

The *best* approach is to be serious but not grave about the situation. Let your kid know you understand that he's scared ("You're really afraid of the pool, aren't you?") You could ask him questions about why he thinks it's scary, not like a prosecutor looking to trip him up, but like a reporter who wants to understand the facts of this situation from his perspective. Who knows, you may be rewarded with a succinct explanation that points to a misperception that can be fixed. If you say to a child who trembles as a fly whizzes by, "Don't be silly, the fly can't hurt you" the child may not believe you. But if you ask why she's afraid and she tells you she's afraid the fly will sting, you can explain that some insects, like bees, can sting but flies can't. If she's three or older, and therefore able to follow your logic (at least some of the time) this might allay her fear.

Even if your child offers no explanation for her worry, it's still worthy of your respect. Perhaps Charlie would have stuck a toe in the pool if his dad had simply said something like "I see the pool looks scary to you," and then told him it was okay to be scared—other children have been scared of water before they learned to swim, too. He could have taken the pressure off by telling Charlie he never, ever had to go into the pool until he was ready. In the meantime, if he wanted, he could just sit and watch the other children.

Doing so would have put Charlie in control of his fear. He'd get to decide when he was ready to conquer it. And with his dad as a sympathetic ally that time might have come before the summer after all.

13. Don't Overreact

My mother, the world's daintiest person, reports that she had scabs on her knees almost continuously until she was old enough for algebra. So you can expect that your children will, too. Getting hurt is an inevitable part of growing up. A parent's job is to make sure that the unavoidable boo-boos of childhood are limited to just that—injuries that can be healed with a bandage and a kiss. It would be irresponsible not to carefully childproof your home, to leave your child unsupervised or to put her in a car without a car seat. But once you have created as safe an environment as you can, you have to let them fall.

Only by experimenting do kids gain the confidence they need to develop their physical abilities. No, you don't let a three-year-old climb a tree. But when a little child falls you don't make a big deal out of it unless the child does. If you pay attention, you can see whether a child is crying because he's really in pain or was just shocked and frightened to suddenly discover the sidewalk rising to meet his face. When a little one falls on her bottom the first thing she is likely to do is to look for your reaction. If she's greeted by a look of fear and horror on your face, she'll conclude she really is as fragile as a china doll and start bawling. If you meet her gaze with a smile and a "Whoopsies!" she'll probably laugh and scamper away again.

Children will inevitably trip. But much more harm will come if you trip up their growing confidence by expressing nervousness about their physical abilities. If a child hears "careful! careful!" when all she's doing is running down the sidewalk, she's going to internalize the fear and concern that goes with that warning. That can hurt her a lot more than any bloody knee she gets if she hits the pavement.

There are few things scarier than sprinting to the E.R. with an injured child in your arms. But you need to find a balance between being cautious and overreacting. After all, you don't want to be the Parent who cried Wolf. If you react with the same intensity to her jumping on your king-sized bed as you do to her touching the stove, the message that stoves are absolutely off limits is less likely to get through loud and clear.

14. Explain Yourself

There are good reasons lurking behind most of the "nos" and "don'ts" uttered by parents of young children. You don't want him to touch the computer keyboard because he could inadvertently delete your document. You don't want him to scratch the dining room table with his fork because it won't look nice anymore. You don't want her to push the button on the dishwasher because you haven't put in the soap yet. Too often, though, when we say no to our kids over things that aren't obvious safety issues for them, like touching something hot or running across the street, we stop before we finish the sentence. We issue the prohibition but not the explanation. It only takes a few more seconds to open your child's eyes to the "whys" behind your "nos." Take that extra time as often as possible.

Giving your child an explanation prevents him from viewing your rules as arbitrary and dictatorial. He may not like them, but over time he sees that you have a reason for them. They are based on the facts of life—if you tip over a juice glass it makes a mess, if you hide Daddy's car keys we can't go to Grandpa's. Explaining why we can or can't, should or shouldn't teaches him the rudiments of cause and effect. It begins to demystify the world for him so he can make decisions for himself based on real understanding.

The only drawback to issuing explanations is that it is also likely to teach children to be inquisitive—even when they're better off not knowing or their question masks some hidden agenda. This is especially true of toddlers, so if you have a two-year-old who goes on "why?" jags be sure to read "Don't Answer All of Their Questions" on p. 69.

15. Do Not Lie to Them

"This won't hurt a bit" can be five of the most destructive words in the English language. They destroy a lot of trust when spoken to a cowering four-year-old whose upper arm has just been drizzled with rubbing alcohol in preparation for The Shot. Yet this lie has been passed down for generations by loving parents who think they are somehow doing their child a favor by pretending a shot is not going to hurt when it will.

It would be wonderful if shots didn't sting, nobody was ever mean to you and hot fudge sundaes lowered your triglycerides. But until wishing makes it so, children are better helped if you gently guide them toward facing life squarely. Otherwise they leave the doctor's office feeling not only achy but also betrayed.

It's no fun being the bad news delivery service for your kid. It's human nature to want to sugarcoat the bitter parts of life. It's hard to admit to yourself that your child is encountering something painful. Sometimes parents lie to their child more as a prayer than out of conviction. But if you aren't up-front with your child you're inevitably going to get caught. One of the worst parts of this is that she'll be less likely to trust you the next time— even if you're telling her the truth. If you promise her that "Mommy will be back soon," but in the past that's been your code word for "here comes the baby-sitter, see you in the a.m., Honey," she will not believe that this time you are really just going to the mailbox on the corner.

Sugarcoat everything for your child and she might conclude that *you* can't handle bad news, which means she will be less likely to tell you hers. This will seriously compromise your ability to guide and protect her. When she's a teen you don't want public service announcements to be all that stands between her and disaster. You want her to feel safe telling you her bad news so you don't have to hear even worse news about her from someone else.

So for everybody's sake teach her to face up to life. If you're leaving for work and won't be back till she's in her Cinderella pajamas don't say "I'm going to work for a little while." Just state the facts: "I'm going to work now—I'll be home after your bath." If the toy your child wants costs more than your mortgage payments tell her it costs too much money. If the cat died, tell her it died—not that it went to sleep.

I'm not suggesting you handle these situations coldly. There are gentle ways to break bad news. But being gentle isn't the same as lying. It means telling your child, if he asks, that yes the shot will probably hurt, and you hope it won't hurt a lot. But you promise it will be over very quickly and that you'll hold him the whole time. It means that when you tell her you'll be working late you let her know that you'll be thinking about her, that you love her and that you will (or hope you will) be able to spend extra time with her soon. Being gentle means that, if possible, you wait to tell her the cat died until you have the time to spend with her, to hold her and to answer her questions.

The bottom line is that when something bad or sad is going to happen to your child your job is not to make it go away but to help her learn to cope with it. You do that by being honest in the kindest way you can. So when the bad thing has passed, when the tears have been wiped away and the needle flicked into the dispenser you say "great job" or "You were so brave!" Most of all, you avoid saying seven more of the most destructive words in the English language: "Now that wasn't so bad, was it?"

16. Only Make Promises You Plan to Keep

A young child's memory often fails her—at least when it comes to your rules about not transporting mud pies through the living room or dunking her teddy into the tub. But the most absent-minded youngster has a memory capacity measurable in gigabytes when it comes to your promises.

It's been six months since your trip to Uncle Steve's office in that old building with a winding staircase and gleaming brass banister. Now you're back. "Mommy I want to slide down the railing," your four-year-old announces. Oh no, you say. "But you *promised*! It's not crowded now," wails your offspring. Well, yes you did promise. Half a year ago when he demanded a slide down that banister you held his hand tight and said, "It's too crowded now. Next time, next time, I promise," and quickly distracted him with the revolving door. You did this because at the time he was so hungry and exhausted that he was looking for any excuse to let loose a high-decibel, highly public tantrum. Besides, you didn't think he'd really remember your promise. Try explaining all of this to a four-year-old and come out with your credibility intact.

Between parent and young child acting trustworthy is definitely not a two-way street. They, of course, break their promises to us all the time. They promise they'll still eat their dinner if we let them have pudding first. They promise they'll go right to bed after just one more story. They promise not to touch any of the buttons. Children quickly forget their promises in part because they have a hard time controlling their impulses. He may *want* to sit still while the dentist looks in his mouth and earnestly believes he will. But he just can't do it. You shouldn't really expect him to.

Little kids have a very fuzzy idea of what a promise is anyway. They don't fully understand the power that the word is supposed to convey. It can be confusing to children who are trying to understand the concept of being trustworthy if you play loosely with the notion. The only way they can learn what it really means to give someone your word is by keeping yours. Having an honest, open relationship with your child starts here.

Don't say "I promise" if you're just trying to placate or extricate yourself from a sticky situation. Substitute other vague phraseology like "we'll see," or "we'll talk about it when you're older," or "hmmm, let me think about that one." Even if you've gotten away with false promises in the past, you will eventually get caught. The look of mistrust and confusion on your progeny's angelic face when he discovers he really isn't going to get to ride the space shuttle next year will lead you to deep self-loathing. So just don't go there. When you say "I promise" to your child, make sure it's ironclad.

Inevitably there will come a time when your solemn promise has to be broken. Perhaps you *did* get circus tickets, but on the big day young Jimmy wakes up with the flu. His fever is 104, his head is throbbing, he can hardly walk. But he doesn't understand why he can't see the clowns tomorrow instead. "You promised!" he wails. There's not much you can do about this situation. Just consider it one of those all-important, character-shaping episodes that he will be better off for having experienced. He'll learn you aren't all-powerful and that sometimes the hand of fate can be harsh. But as long as you generally do keep your promises to him he won't conclude that you can't be trusted.

Be forewarned that even if you are fastidious about keeping your promises and never make one you don't mean, you will still be accused of going back on your word. A child who's angling for a new Super Ninja Ecliptosaur will have a very squishy, self-serving interpretation of your, "We'll see, maybe next time." You'll try to explain what you did say (if you even remember). Your child will insist he is owed this toy—he will quote yourself back to you with the reliability rate of a supermarket tabloid. What are you going to do, sue him? Face it, unless you followed your mother's advice and joined your high school debate team you probably have not developed the verbal-sparring skills necessary to match wits with a modern five-year-old. So don't say, "hmmm," "good point," and "I see." Unless you want to be confronted with more doctored quotes tomorrow and the day after that, just say "no."

17. Stop Apologizing for Everything

Even when you are everybody's apple dumpling life doesn't always go your way. Sometimes the cookies are all gone, you have to leave the playground and Daddy needs to talk on the phone rather than to you. Coping with disappointment, much less learning patience, is tough for the stroller set. It is frustrating to have your desires thwarted, to get the inkling that maybe the sun doesn't rise and set on your command. No wonder that when we deliver bad news to children we so often punctuate it with an apology: "I'm sorry, but it's Ginny's turn to ride the swing." "I'm sorry, you can't have ice cream before dinner." "I'm sorry, you can't bop your sister on the head with your stegosaurus."

Sweetening up bad news by attaching an apology might seem like a good idea at first. After all, it's a form of respecting the child, of acknowledging his feelings and the disappointment he's about to face. The problem is that it sends some additional messages you probably didn't intend. Are you really sorry that Ethan can't try to crack his sister's head open with his toy? By apologizing you imply that there is some hardship involved in following basic rules of decorum—and that you are somehow to blame for enforcing them. Young children readily connect the concept of "saying you're sorry" with being at fault. They are asked to pronounce those magic words every time they encroach on some other child's rights—usually by hitting, kicking or perpetrating other physical violence. So when a parent keeps apologizing the child gets the idea that the parent is somehow to blame for everything.

In some cases, apologizing also sends your child the message that he deserves special treatment. "I'm sorry I can't talk to you right now, I'm on the phone." "I'm sorry you can't have candy right now." "I'm sorry I have to go to work." The implication of all of these is that your child is not just at the center of your life, but at the center of the universe.

If you find yourself apologizing to your child to the point of obsequiousness remind yourself that it's your job to be the powerful one. It does a child little good (and much harm) if you hand that power over to him through constant apologies. It may be unfortunate from your child's standpoint that he has to give Ginny a turn on the swing. But he isn't owed an apology for being made to do the right thing.

An occasional apology isn't likely to create a God complex in your child. But beware if you find yourself apologizing for everything—even the weather. Part of the problem may be semantics. Often we use "I'm sorry" as a short cut for "it may be regrettable to you, but . . ." a phrase that is unlikely to trip off the tongue when discoursing with a wailing two-year-old. The solution is not to start speaking to your child in a stilted manner, but simply to stifle the apology. Instead, issue a simple directive: "Time to stop swinging now and give Ginny a turn." "You can have ice cream *after* dinner." "No! You may not hit Abigail with your dinosaur!" You can acknowledge your child's disappointment, but not by apologizing. Substitute a simple, "Oh well," or "Gee, you're really angry about this, aren't you?"

If you're a habitual apologizer, take it from an old pro: You won't be able to quash the "sorrys" overnight. The first step is just to pay attention to what you say, and become aware of how often, and in which contexts, you imply self-blame when you announce bad news. You can then correct yourself by adding a more accurate assessment of the situation like, "that's too bad," a note of sympathy that doesn't lead the child to conclude that you're responsible for his mess—or the universe's.

17 1/2. But Say You're Sorry When You Should Be

It's destructive to apologize to children when life happens. But when you *are* the screw-up there is nothing more powerful you can say to your child than a simple, "I'm sorry." In fact, the worst part of making a mistake as a parent isn't usually the mistake itself, but not owning up to it.

"Don't touch the milk," you tell three-year-old Nate before leaving the kitchen for a millisecond, which is just long enough for the milk carton to spill. You come back to find Nate gleefully slogging through the puddle in his slippers. Since you're too sleep-deprived to spell the word patience, much less act it out, you go ballistic—screaming "no, no, no! We don't spill milk!" You put Nate in time-out, and, what with him screaming and you desperately trying to mop up the mess, it's a few moments before you hear your six-year-old daughter's eyewitness account. Only then do you discover that the true culprit was Misha the cat—who is now atop the china cabinet, licking her fur in as blasé a fashion as she can muster.

In a scenario like this it's going to make a big difference to teary-eyed Nate whether you look at him and say, "Well, let that be a lesson to *you* not to spill milk," or give him a heartfelt hug and kiss and say, "Oh, I'm so sorry Nate. Mommy made a mistake."

By apologizing you not only help to heal Nate's hurt feelings but teach him other valuable Life Lessons. Saying "I'm sorry" shows your child you respect him—that he is someone worthy of apologizing to when you make a mistake in his direction. Since little kids are, well, very little and we are very big in comparison, they swell up with pride when we treat them like they are important. Respect your child and he'll come to respect himself. Think how you'd feel if a stranger almost punctured your foot with her stiletto heel on a crowded rush-hour bus and then didn't apologize. You'd seethe not just because your foot ached but because the lack of apology suggested a callous disregard for your personhood. Put a young child in the same situation and he or she may not know enough to be angry at the lack of respect. That's because young children are just learning what their place in the world is and the rules of conduct between them and other people. You certainly don't want to give them the impression that it's okay for them to be hurt, falsely accused or maligned without it meaning much to anyone.

Saying you're sorry doesn't just teach your children self-respect—it teaches them to respect other people as well. Children learn a lot through imitation—they model themselves after us. So by apologizing you teach your children to say they're sorry when they make a mistake. By not apologizing you send the message that your child isn't worth very much, and that other people aren't of much value either.

When you apologize for your mistakes you're also passing on to your child the whole "buck stops here" tradition of taking responsibility for your actions. This will serve her well whether she grows up to be President or someone wearing stiletto heels on a crowded bus. Being a stand-up kind of person is one of the moral foundations of civilized behavior and a prerequisite for any kind of self-knowledge and growth. Think about it—if you're raised in a house where people don't own up to their mistakes you're likely to inter- nalize that approach to life. That means you'll spend your life blaming every- one and everything for your errors (I just have bad luck, the dog ate it, the light was green, he walked into my knife) instead of admitting your own guilt.

The biggest problem with this approach is that you never get to benefit from your mistakes. You get the hardship and inconvenience they cause, but because you're so busy disowning them you don't get the learning curve they offer. Jan and Tammy both give lousy presentations to the company president. Jan blames her assistant for refusing to work overtime and help her, her boss for giving poor guidance, her office mate for deliberately steering her wrong in order to make himself look good. Meanwhile, Tammy blames herself. Whose next presentation will be much improved? Tammy's of course. Jan will be too busy bemoaning her boss, her secretary and her back-stabbing co-worker—everyone but the one person who can improve the situation, herself.

But probably the best reason to apologize to your child for your gaffes is that it's an admission of your imperfection. And from a child's eye view, if you accept your own mistakes with good grace you're likely to do the same for hers. Translation: The child learns that your love for her isn't conditional on her being perfect. She can be woefully flawed and lovable all at the same time—and there's no better legacy you can give a child than that.

18. Never Force-Feed Them

Before I was a mother I actually believed those nutritionists who blame parents for their children's finicky eating habits. Some even theorize that the only reason young children will voraciously polish off a scoop of Rocky Road but shun their salad is the context in which these foods are offered by Dad or (usually) Mom. The supposed problem is that vegetables are presented as something you must eat and ice cream as a special treat. By accentuating the difference between the two we program our children to prefer the sugary and fatty over the lean and green. The supposed solution is to offer kids broccoli with great fanfare, even give it for dessert! If we imbue it with all of the positive psychological nuances we reserve for sweets our children will eventually crave it as much as sugar cookies.

Meanwhile, back on planet Earth most parents know the typical child cannot be tricked into feeling about peas and carrots what he does for birthday cake. Children tend to be disdainful of bitter foods and full of craving for the sweet and the sinful. Perhaps there is some evolutionary basis for this. Whatever its root, this preference for sweet and/or fatty foods is undeniably powerful.

Eventually, however, most kids can develop an interest, or at least a tolerance, for foods that come in various hues of green and orange, if you gently but consistently offer them on a daily basis. Getting your child to eat what's good for them takes diplomacy. If you are authoritarian about the consumption of broccoli your child is likely to develop an aversion to it. When I was a child my mother actually believed her friends who claimed *their* children were culinary adventurers. No matter what gourmet concoctions her friends dreamt up their children would eat it—even if it contained mushrooms. So, my otherwise extraordinarily kindhearted mother got the notion in her head that if all these other children were happily eating mushrooms, *her* children should at least be willing to try, say, blueberries. Five of these purple, pea-sized, and to my mind extremely suspicious-looking berries were presented to me at lunch. I balked, she insisted. I can't remember how many hours (in her defense, it was probably minutes) I had to sit there or whether I ever ate a single one, but I know we both learned a lesson—she learned not to believe her friends and I learned never to eat blueberries.

If you get into a power struggle with your kids over food you lose even if you win. You may get them to swallow the food once, or even ten times. But they won't feel good about it, which means eating it won't become a habit. Since that's the goal, being tactful and sly is the proper strategy. Don't insist they eat green stuff, but present it to them in small portions over and over again. Somedays they'll ignore it, other days they'll pick at it, on occasion they may actually eat it. By using this sort of approach my friend Katie has produced a son who, at age five, proclaims that kale is his favorite food. That's a high mark to aim for. For myself, I'll be satisfied if decades hence the vegetable bin in my daughter's refrigerator is not used to store Spam and Miracle Whip.

19. Ignore the Potty Wars

The experts are duking it out. For the last 30 or so years American children have been waving goodbye to diapers later and later. In the early '60s, 90 percent of 2½ year olds had made the transition to the toilet. By the late 1990s that figure had plummeted to a mere 10 percent. Some lay the blame at the feet of experts, most notably Harvard's T. Berry Brazelton, M.D., who advocates letting the child decide when he's ready to stop wearing diapers. But it could just as easily be due to technical advancements in disposable diapers which have made them so comfortable kids have less incentive to give them up. Whatever the cause of this change, there is now a backlash—a small but potentially growing chorus of experts who say there's something amiss when 3 1/2-year-olds aren't using a potty yet.

Who's right? It doesn't matter. Childrearing trends come and go. What's important is what works with *your* child. Feel free to experiment. You can try the long, drawn-out "toilet teaching" method where you introduce the potty and let him stare at it forever if necessary before you gingerly suggest he *use* it. Or you can try the quick and very dirty "toilet training" method of letting him go around bare-bottomed for about a week until he finally agrees with you that the potty is a better place for that stuff to end up than his legs and the floor. There's nothing wrong with waiting till a child is ready. Just keep in mind that the arrival of that magical day will depend in part on the decisions *you* make—including whether you leave your wood floors bare or have them expensively carpeted and whether you use disposable diapers or leakier cloth ones.

What's most important, no matter which approach you take, is that you not *force* your child. If your method of choice doesn't work, try another approach instead. Often the best strategy is simply to wait, even if that means you end up with one of those kids who's still in diapers when all of her friends have graduated to Minnie Mouse undies. For too many kids the potty becomes the ultimate symbol of parental power. It represents all of those things you make them do—like wear their mittens and brush their teeth— that they really would rather not. If they see it's of great importance to you that they use it, they may be less likely to.

The most important part of choosing a potty method is not to be doctrinaire. Don't put the theories ahead of common sense. For example, the pediatrician kept advising Penny not to pressure her daughter Dana to use the potty—otherwise Dana might initiate a power struggle over the issue, which would mean it would take even longer before she learned. Penny had no difficulty following this advice when Dana was two and even three, especially since it seemed to be working. By her third birthday Dana always urinated in the potty and was dry every night. But she still insisted on being diapered when she needed to move her bowels.

By the time Dana's fourth birthday was approaching and she was still pooping in diapers, Penny became concerned. The pediatrician kept warning her to leave Dana alone. Finally, Penny got a second opinion from a child psychologist who suspected that Dana was refusing to poop in the toilet simply because she was afraid. She recommended that Penelope talk to Dana about her upcoming birthday and tell her firmly but delicately that it was time to stop being afraid of the toilet and that Mommy would help her. For one more week she could use diapers, Penny explained, and then it would be time to throw them all away. When the big day came Dana cried that she didn't want to use the toilet, but eventually she did. After her first success she never asked for diapers again. She was trained in a day. That night she even thanked her mother for helping her and talked about what a big girl she had become.

By eschewing the standard wisdom, Penny not only got her daughter out of diapers but also helped her see that she could overcome a fear. The approach she used wouldn't be right for every preschooler who's still in diapers, but it was right for Dana—and that's the whole point. When it comes to toilet training, teaching or whatever, the best approach is always the one that works best for *your* child, no matter what the experts are proclaiming this week.

20. Don't Answer
All of Their Questions

If your child is typical your daily life is punctuated by a simple refrain: "Why?" On some days there is nothing more adorable than that question being asked over and over again in a sweet little squeaky voice. But on other days it can drive you nuts. Little children ask why for the very simple reason that there's so much about life that they just don't get. How else are they going to understand the world unless you guide them toward the answers? Like a hearty appetite, a hearty curiosity is a wonderful thing in young children. It means they're off to a good start, foraging for all the "brain food" they need to develop their knowledge base and cognitive skills. You don't want to be dismissive ("Just because," "I don't know," "Go ask your father") because you want to encourage them to ask questions and get their brain wheels used to doing a lot of turning. You want to celebrate their curiosity by answering their questions as best you can.

But there comes a point—and I'm sure you've already been there. Sometimes explaining things to your child is just not the best strategy. As a parent you learn to separate the "why" that should be respected and answered clearly and thoughtfully from the "why" that deserves something else. Such as when:

1. Your child really doesn't want to know why. This is usually the case when you get caught up in a round robin:

Two-year-old: "Why do birds fly?"
You: "Because that's how they get around."
Two-year-old: "Why?"
You: "So they can look for food."
Two-year-old: "Why?"
You: "So they can eat."
Two-year-old: "Why?"
You: "To keep healthy and strong."
Two-year-old: "Why?"
You: "So they can fly."
Two-year-old: "Why ?"
You: "To look for food."

This child doesn't want to know why birds fly as much as she wants to have a conversation with her mommy. She keeps saying "why" to keep the conversation going. So if you distract her by giving her another form of attention, you can break out of the "why loop." You can ask her why *she* thinks birds fly, or suggest that the two of you look at her bird book or look out the window together to watch birds. Of course, if she stubbornly keeps asking you why birds fly she really does want to know, so now is a great opportunity to expand her mind by explaining it to her as best you can.

2. You're just completely exhausted and think you will go out of your mind if she asks why one more time. In this case, distraction is the best strategy—or an honest explanation of your current state of mind, combined with a promise to discuss it with her later.

3. Your answer will scare your child. As much as you want to expand your child's mind, there are some things that are better left unsaid. You don't tell a three-year-old with a serious food allergy that eating a peanut might kill him. You tell him that he's allergic to peanuts so he shouldn't eat any or he will get sick. You don't go into gory details

about why he shouldn't talk to strangers. You say it's not safe to because they may not be nice even though they seem to be. Sometimes you have to protect your child from his own curiosity.

4. When "why?" is really a challenge to your authority. It's easy to spot this because the "why?" usually comes out as "Whyyyyyyyyy?" As in:

You: Clean up time now.
Yours: Whyyyyyyyyyyy?
You: Because play time is over.
Yours: Whyyyyyyyyyyy?
You: Because we have to get ready for dinner.
Yours: Whyyyyyyyyyyy?

Obviously, this child is not really asking, he's protesting. When met with such whining should you supply your child with answers? Of course not. You should supply your child with *one* answer: the traditional parent fallback, passed down through millennia for the simple reason that it works:

You: Because I say so.

21. Give In

You can't always get what you want, but it's human nature to want what you can't have. This fact of life inevitably creates a dilemma for parents who, in their wisdom, would prefer their children's lives be devoid of violent TV shows, candy, and dolls whose proportions don't bare even a vague resemblance to a living, breathing female. Sometimes, the more you say no the more desperately your child longs for you to say yes.

Your first line of defense should be to mount a strong offense. Being a control freak makes sense when you have a two-year-old. For as long as it works, simply keep him away from anything you'd prefer he not encounter. He won't be aware that he is deliberately being deprived of watching shoot-em-ups or eating fast-food burgers.

But eventually (this is what play dates and older cousins are infamous for) your offspring will discover that some cereal is pink and tastes as sweet as it looks and that the TV can be set at a channel other than the one reserved for PBS. Often, at least at first, you can quash his requests to bring these pleasures into your home by simply stating your position. "No toy guns allowed," "We don't watch those TV shows," etc. Give honest explanations for your rules—i.e., "It's not healthy," "Too much fighting," "It's not good for you." There are parents who can get away with this approach for extended periods of time—even two months. But more likely your child will soon become dogged in his constant pleading and begging for you to change your mind.

If distraction and feigning deafness don't work, there's only one approach left: caving. If there's something your child craves you have no other choice, unless it would create a true health or safety risk. You may not relish the notion of your child spending even a millisecond watching Batman cartoons. But your goal is to prevent him from spending every waking hour yearning for the Dynamic Duo. This is far more likely if you deprive him of them completely. The forbidden is always enticing. Allow it and you strip it of its allure. This isn't a perfect solution since it won't keep your child away from bad influences. But it will prevent him from being subsumed by them.

No, you should not stop imposing your values on your kids. But you can find ways to compromise. Perhaps they only watch those dreaded TV shows a couple of times a week. Or, they have dessert at the doughnut shop on occasion. If you think colored cereal is really candy, buy it anyway, but insist your kids eat it instead of candy, not instead of breakfast. Most likely, after a few days of gorging themselves on chartreuse marshmallows the "cereal" box will languish on the pantry shelf. But they may still check on it every once in a while just to make sure it's still there.

22. Let Them Be Babyish

Almost all children have an inner drive to grow up. You need to have some fire in your belly to learn how to walk, talk and take apart Dad's alarm clock. Having high expectations of your kids will give them even more incentive to accomplish more and more every day. But growing up is pretty heady stuff. Sometimes it can become so overwhelming a child needs to run for cover, take a step backwards. This is commonly known as regression— you can see it in the three-year-old who starts substituting karate chops for words, rather than the other way around, or who suddenly wants to use a bottle, sit in his little sister's high chair and carry around his blanket again.

Episodes of this sort are not at all uncommon during early childhood. Often they occur when the child is feeling stressed out, when he's becoming a big brother or sister, moving to a new home, starting a new school, etc. But sometimes there's no clear explanation other than growing pains. For ten days four-year-old Max seemed like a basket case to his mom. Suddenly he was crying when she dropped him off at preschool—just the way he had when he was two. He talked baby talk at home and dragged his old teddy bear out of the closet. His parents couldn't figure out what had gotten into him. Nothing had changed at home or at school to trigger his reaction. While they were still trying to decide what to do about the new Baby Max, he suddenly started acting like a four-year-old again. Only now his preschool teacher reported that he seemed far more attentive and was doing much better at sharing and taking turns. At home, he even let his little brother play with his prized space shuttle model—an unprecedented act of generosity. In retrospect his parents realized that Max had to go into reverse for a little while to rev his engines. Sometimes kids have to take a few steps backwards before they make a major leap forward.

The best way to help a child who stops acting his age is to indulge him. If he can still fit in that high chair, let him in for dessert. Don't chide or tease him for wanting his teddy bear or sippy cup again. You don't have to let this go on forever, but a week or so won't hurt. You can even tell him that he can have his bottle back for a specific (short) period of time, and then it will be time to put it away again.

Since his desire to go backwards may indicate anxiety about going forwards, you should also pump him up about growing up. Let him know how proud you are of him. Point out all of the things he can do now that a younger child couldn't. If there aren't any benefits to getting bigger in your home, maybe it's time to loosen up. His regression may actually be a sign that you're treating him like a younger child than he is now ready to be. So, for example, consider letting him stay up later than he used to, turn on the dishwasher himself, go to preschool for more days, etc.

If the regression lasts more than a couple of weeks it could be a sign of excess stress he just can't handle. Take a close look at his life and do what you can to alleviate whatever pressure he's under. Sometimes, however, kids get stuck in a regression because of the way Mom or Dad responds to it. Be sure you're not scolding him for wanting time off from growing up. Longing for the good old days is a common and normal desire—even if you're a two-year-old.

23. Don't Make Fun of Them

"Look Mommy, a cantaloupe!" Bystanders at the zoo start to giggle at your three-year-old's malapropism. She looks around, confused. Why is everybody laughing at her? It's in her best interest if, when she looks up at you, she doesn't see a look of hilarity on your face as well. She will be much better off if you can say lovingly, with a straight face, "Yes, I see the *antelope*, darling."

Most parents know not to laugh when their child is injured or afraid. But giggles can hurt at other times, too. We all know there's a difference between laughing *with* and laughing *at* someone. If you constantly poke fun at a child's shortcomings, no matter how adorable, she will feel devalued—like a pet or this afternoon's entertainment. It's unlikely she will be able to tell you she feels humiliated. But over time you will be able to tell from her behavior that she considers it her role to be cute—and that will get tiring for all involved very quickly. The antidote is to treat her with respect—to respond to her errors and misconceptions in a loving, straightforward manner, rather than as a source of amusement.

You won't always be able to do this. A young child's misconceptions are so precious and priceless you will be tempted to have her repeat them in the presence of her grandparents. I think the most amusing errors kids make are word replacements (for example, always referring to a baby-sitter as "my baby sister") and using common expressions in their own way. You get stopped at a red light and your two-year-old says with a dramatic sigh, "I just hate when this happens." "Ohmigod, Mommy, this is sooooo funny," says your three-year-old "Valley Girl." "I'm gonna make your day," says your five-year-old, squinty-eyed, to a friend he's play-fighting with. "Whoever heard of such a crazy thing?" your four-year-old says when informed it's time for his bath. Maybe his words sound adorably crazy to you, but try to keep your opinion to yourself.

24. Think Like a Kid

It's a watershed moment in your life as a parent when your child finally hits an age that you recall being. Memories of your nursery school teacher's perfume, or the way your first Barbie's hair flipped may be sharply etched into your mind. So are certain feelings you had—the hurt when you were falsely accused of breaking a lamp, the pride when your mom played the piano for your class, the unshakable belief that on your birthday, at least, you stood at the center of all creation. These memories add resonance to your experience as a parent and also offer you a powerful parenting tool. They help you retain at least traces of what it feels like to be a kid. The result is that you can communicate with your own more effectively.

Of course, the four-year-old you're dealing with now is your child, not a clone. So you can't expect her to think and feel exactly like you did. But there are some fundamentals about childhood. So remember these basics of kidthink:

I Have My Reasons.

No matter how bizarro my behavior seems, I'm not being irrational—I'm just misinformed. Three-year-old Olivia announced that she did not want to go to sleep, she was not tired. "Stay in your bed," her father warned. As soon as he turned his back, she snuck into the kitchen and grabbed a carrot. "Back in your bed," he ordered and asked her to put the carrot back. But she would not let it go. Instead, Olivia dashed off into her bedroom, buried herself under the blankets and started munching on the carrot. "No eating in bed, Olivia!" her father said. Olivia started to cry. Her father held her until her sobs turned into dry heaves and then subsided. Finally she told him the truth. She was afraid of the dark. She overheard Mommy telling her big brother that carrots help you see better at night, so that's why she had to have one. Her dad suggested a nightlight instead, and Olivia finally went to sleep.

I'm a literalist.

Say "that's a good way to get your hands dirty" to a three-year-old who's about to dig bare-handed for worms and you'll confuse him. He's *supposed* to do "good" things isn't he? So does Mommy think it's good for him to get his hands dirty? Then why is she frowning?

I can believe two contradictory notions at the same time.

I know super heroes aren't real but I will still ask, "Daddy, other than Superman, is there anyone in the world stronger than you?" This is one reason why a dose of reality does not eradicate a child's fears. A little boy or girl can know that the bogeyman isn't real and still be convinced he's under the bed. Children know they can't fly—but you still need to install window guards.

I don't always put the feelings into my words.

"You don't like me, Mommy," says your four-year-old from her time-out chair. She says it so simply, so matter-of-factly that at first you might assume there's not a lot of emotion behind her thought. But kids will do this—suddenly express a fear or worry so straightforwardly that it sounds superficial. Instead of a pat, "Of course I do" these utterances should be handled with the same sensitivity and respect you would muster if she said it with her voice quivering. Sit down beside her, put an arm around her and say, "I do like you. I love you. But I don't like what you did. You're having a time-out because you threw your puzzle across the room when I told you it was time to clean up. But Mommy loves you even when you do something wrong."

Life as we know it revolves around me.

No matter how much evidence suggests otherwise, the typical, well-loved child will assume that the important grownups in her life exist solely for her benefit. She just doesn't get that they are independent people who, for all their love of her, also have other things and people to think about, worry about, care for and enjoy—including themselves.

I'm unpredictable.

Sometimes, no matter what you do you can't get him to behave. As soon as his punishment is over he proceeds to kick his brother again. And then, one day, all you have to do is utter a quiet "that's enough now" and an era of peace descends on your household for an unprecedented twenty-five minutes.

I can't wait.

It's unbearable, impossible, I won't do it, can't do it. It has to be NOW!!!!!!!!!!!!!!!!!!

But when you're in a rush I have plenty of time.

I couldn't tell you if twenty seconds have passed since I started looking at this book or twenty minutes. I don't remember if I last fed my goldfish this morning or yesterday. I will ask you how many days until my birthday almost every day. A child's sense of time has, at best, a tenuous relationship with the earth's rotation. Even if they are precocious enough to decipher a clock face they still don't understand the concept of time passing. Left to themselves the only clock to which they adhere is their body's. They know it's dinnertime or snacktime when they are hungry. Naptime or bedtime when they are tired. Generally, time falls into two categories for young kids—too short and too long. Play time is too short. Mommy talking on the phone is *always* too long.

25. Tell Them about Your Childhood

No self-respecting teenager would sit still for a conversation that begins, "Back in my day . . ." But young children are likely to be fascinated by stories about your childhood. It amuses—and comforts—them to envision you once as they are now, grappling with the big world just like they have to. Your son will feel a sense of pride that he's so much like his daddy was at his age. Over time, identifying with his parents and grandparents will add to his sense of who he is and the legacy that comes to him by virtue of being your child (I'm adventurous like all the Ross's, I'm generous like Grandpa was).

Talking about your own childhood offers an additional benefit. It gives you a somewhat subtle forum for giving little children advice. (I say "somewhat" because with little children you have to be careful about being too subtle— they can miss your point altogether.) Here's how you can best use your own past to help your children find solutions to troubles they are having in the present:

Be selective.

Keep in mind when combing your childhood for material that your child is not yet ready for the unexpurgated version. There's no need to divulge that pea soup always made you puke, that you landed your brother in the emergency room three times or got kicked out of nursery school for biting.

Embellish.

Customize your story to fit their current dilemma. Tell your younger daughter how you handled getting your feelings hurt by your big sister. Tell her what Grandma told you and what you did. Even if you don't remember feeling as timid as your child on the first day of school, you can still claim that you were as scared as she is. Then tell her how much fun you had when you finally got there. Likewise, if your son is having problems sleeping because his teddy bear got left in the hotel room in Boca you can tell him that when you were his age you had a—guess what—little panda bear just like his, also named Bamboo, that got lost. You were very sad, but then after a good cry you decided to be brave and go to sleep holding onto your blanket instead. And you did it! Then you can offer to tuck him in. There's no guarantee he'll be as flexible as you supposedly were as a three-year-old, but he certainly won't roll his eyes at your blatant attempt to manipulate him. More likely he'll be transfixed by it. You have enormous clout in his book, so hearing that you understand what he's feeling and have experienced it yourself will bring him plenty of comfort.

End happily.

Make sure your little tale ends on an up note, with you triumphing over adversity. On occasion, of course, you'll want to tell some not-so-happy tales. For example, you can emphasize a safety rule by mentioning the sad story of cousin Larry whose fingers really did get slammed by the car door and had to be fixed at the hospital. But for the most part it's wiser to use your childhood reminiscences to inspire rather than to scare.

Remember what you told them.

Two months from now your son may request that you repeat the story of your lost panda. Unbeknownst to you he has been pondering the fate of Bamboo on and off over the past weeks and has some questions. He'll want to know the panda's last name, and whether Grandma looked under the hotel bed and if not, couldn't Bamboo still be there? Shouldn't you call the hotel to check? When he comes to you with these grave questions it's best if your reaction isn't "Huh? What panda?"

Chapter Two

RULES FOR THE AGES

BABIES

Spoil Them

Actually, you *can't* spoil a baby. But plenty of parents fear that you can. They try very hard to be strict and rigid with their infants and end up creating a lot of misery for everyone. Here are some of the ways parents have believed erroneously you could spoil a baby:

- Picking her up every time she cries.
- Rocking her to sleep.
- Feeding her whenever she's hungry.
- Playing with her whenever she's in the mood.
- Carrying her around a lot, even when she's not asking you to.

When people say these things spoil a baby, what they really mean is that they create "bad habits" by raising high expectations of Mom and Dad that you will eventually be too exhausted to meet. If you spoil a baby she won't learn to be independent. You'll always have to rock her to sleep. She'll grow up to be a cry baby, etc.

The plain truth is, she's less likely to grow up to be a cry baby if you don't try to stop her from being a cry baby now when she's *supposed* to be one. In other words, you don't spoil children by responding lovingly and diligently to the needs they have that make sense for the age they are now. To get clichéd about it, crying a lot and wanting to be held and carried are "age appropriate" for infants. Babies are wired to ask you to do these things for them because they need these things to happen in order for them to grow optimally. They tend to get stuck at these stages if their needs aren't met—if you try *not* to spoil them.

Look at it from the baby's perspective. One minute you're in this nice warm womb where you can hear your mommy's soothing heartbeat. You're never too hot or cold. You're never hungry. You get carried everywhere. You can sleep whenever you want. And then, suddenly, you get booted out. You're in a strange, confusing place which over-taxes your senses. There are strange new things to touch, smell and see, new sensations to feel. It's hard to process all of these experiences because you don't yet understand that you are a "you" much less perceive that what you're feeling is pain in your tummy because you're hungry. So you do what you've been biologically programmed to do—you cry. What happens next is going to go a very long way in determining your opinion of the new world. If suddenly something soft and warm is put in your mouth to suck which miraculously soothes your stomach, you're going to feel pretty good about this new place. Or at least you'll be willing to give it a chance. But if very often your cries are not met with the kind of comforting you need, whether you're hungry or scared, or want to be held, you're less likely to have a positive attitude.

This is the difference between getting a child off to a good start or a shaky one. And as momentous as this is for a baby, it's relatively simple for parents. Don't worry about habits. Babies may get into them, but infants are pretty pliable. You can ease a baby out of a habit when you need to—as long as you don't need to until he or she is old enough. If you have one of those adaptable babies who is happy being put on a schedule early on and that suits your needs, congratulations. But if you have the more typical baby who is not, pick him up and hold him whenever he cries for you. Feed him when he's hungry.

As the baby grows, many of his needs will cease to be such a dramatic emergency to him. He'll be able to wait without turning appalling shades of purple while you prepare his bottle. He'll be able to fall asleep peacefully without being rocked (he may not *want* to fall asleep this way, but he can do it without feeling traumatized). No one can tell you when this will happen for your baby. It certainly won't be at two days, and it will probably be before six months. The point is that there's no need to stop rocking him at three days because you're worried you'll still be doing it at three years. You won't because you will know better. You can't spoil a baby. But you *can* spoil a three-year-old.

Be Consistent

Among the most popular gifts for new parents are those books that tell you what to expect once the baby finally arrives. These tomes soon become dog-eared from frequent reading because *not* knowing what to expect means there's one thing you can anticipate for sure: plenty of anxiety. Knowing what lies ahead helps you cope. Unfortunately, there's no primer available for the person who is truly clueless about what to expect—the baby. The only way he's going to learn what to expect from the world is by learning what to expect from you.

If you pick him up every time he cries, he'll come to count on comfort. Feed him quickly when he's hungry and he'll assume happily that he will always be nourished. By creating a warm nest of consistent care for him you make the transition from womb to world much easier. And you also create a firm foundation on which he can build his understanding of what it means to be in this strange new place. I'm not advocating one specific kind of routine. Having your expectations met—your food comes when you're hungry, Daddy sings to you when you're sleepy—gives you a foundation for future learning because it allows you to make assumptions about the world. All babies are little scientists, which means they naturally try to explore the world and make hypotheses about it that they then test (Will Mommy make that funny face if I drop my bottle again? Will she pick me up if I cry?). If the baby is always left guessing, his confidence that he can ever begin to understand the world is going to be pretty low.

Being consistent with a baby means trying to instill within him good expectations of the world. It doesn't mean you have to set his feeding and sleeping on a strict schedule. It's no great catastrophe if lunch comes at noon one day and at 1:00 P.M. the next. But if each day it falls somewhere between ten and three that's too much variety. Likewise, don't keep him up until midnight one night, then ask him to go down at eight the next.

Of course, babies vary greatly in how much they crave routine—some are more rigid, others more flexible. What is probably most important is that you try to be consistent when it comes to your emotional responses. Babies come to read faces and emotions through intense observation. If some mornings you look bright and cheerful hovering over her crib and other mornings you are silently morose she won't know what to expect when your shadow looms over her tomorrow.

If you're moody by nature you can't necessarily change your personality now—and you certainly don't want to act around your child as if you're on happy pills or living in Stepford. But you can modulate your emotions somewhat. Try to make an effort to be consistent (in a happy way) for your baby's sake. (If you're moodiness is tied to emotional troubles or substance abuse, seek help for *everybody's* sake.)

Studies show that babies whose needs are responded to on a consistent basis have what experts call a secure attachment to their mother or whoever is taking care of them most of the time. This means they feel connected and safe, which is supposed to be a harbinger of growing up to be a relatively happy, well-adjusted person. Those whose needs aren't met tend to be poorly attached, which some experts believe makes it a struggle for them to make connections with other people as they grow up. Those whose needs are met inconsistently tend to be insecurely attached—which means, basically, that they feel insecure. And since the world offers most of us plenty of unmeetable challenges, bad luck and broken pretzels it helps to at least start out with some modicum of confidence that you can handle what life dishes out.

Talk to Them

Thanks to advances in neurobiology we now know that infants are born with use-it-or-lose-it brains. Mental development depends not just on the quantity of gray matter, but on how frequently—and early in life—your brain is stimulated. That means babies' brains come pre-packaged to absorb and understand language, provided they get the proper exposure to the spoken word. Nature wouldn't make something that's so crucial to a child's development difficult for parents to accomplish. So stimulating the language center in your child's brain is breathtakingly simple. You don't have to buy any special toys or tapes. You just have to have conversations with your baby from the very beginning, even though he obviously can't hold up his end of the dialogue.

As easy as talking to a baby is, some parents don't do it enough simply because they are unaware of its importance. Since most babies don't talk in their first year of life, it's easy to assume they can't understand or benefit from anything you say to them. And, too, when you're so bleary-eyed from lack of sleep that aiming spoonfuls of rice cereal at that little mouth is challenging enough, talking about it is probably the last thing you want to do.

If you find talking to your baby awkward, silly, boring or you're so exhausted the sound of your own voice is grating to your ears, the following research findings should galvanize you to yak away anyway. Babies are able to process language almost from the get go—actually from *before* the get-go. Research finds that newborns prefer the sound of their own mother's voice to other sounds, suggesting that they've been listening to her talk from inside the womb. For the same reason, studies find that at *two days old* babies can tell the difference between the sounds commonly found in their language vs a foreign one. Long before the first "dada" or "banana" the typical baby is breaking up the sounds she hears into words, phrases and clauses. At four months a baby can tell when a spoken clause is beginning and ending, even if he or she can't understand the words. By nine months babies can tell where words begin and end and some can understand as many as a hundred words. So if your baby's entire vocabulary still consists of "ga" remember that still waters run deep.

Babies don't necessarily talk sooner if you converse with them a lot. But they will understand more. This is called receptive language—and it's pretty much ground zero in terms of your child's future verbal development. It doesn't matter what your baby can say. It does matter what he or she can understand. Pediatricians say parents are hyper-focused on a child's first words and tend to worry if their child is slow to talk. It's understandable why parents wait so expectantly for their little one to speak. We erroneously connect early talking with intelligence. Babies who are precocious in this area are presumed to be future academic stars while those who are late speakers are assumed to be less bright. It's just not so.

Let's be blunt: Some people are smarter than others, for whatever reason. So it stands to reason that some babies are smarter than others as well. But you can't tell a baby's future intelligence by when he or she begins to speak. There are so many variables other than pure brain power that factor into it, including the environment, genetics (for example, tongue and mouth muscles may develop sooner in one child than another), gender (girls have an edge here, the extent of which is debatable), personality (some bolder babies jump right in with "to" for "stroller," others don't try until they can muster a closer approximation). Arguably, a child who begins to talk early, formulates phrases and sentences early, *and* understands language beyond what her peers can process, is likely to be on the bright side. But a child who doesn't could be equally bright, brighter, average or dull. You just don't know.

You can't turn your child into someone she isn't meant to be. But you can help her maximize the brain she was born with. One of the most crucial ways you do that is to raise her from the start in a home that helps her learn language.

How do you get babies to understand speech? One thing you don't do is stick them in front of a TV and expect them to learn English from Elmo. Scientists actually tried that with babies whose parents were hearing impaired. It didn't help. What a baby needs is a language partner with whom to have conversations. This might sound like a contradiction. How can you carry on a conversation with someone who can't talk? You do it by offering up soliloquies that focus on what you're doing with the baby, peppered with questions for him or her that you answer yourself. Here's a sample script.

Mom: Okay sweetie pie, are you ready for your cereal? (pause)
Baby: Aba.
Mom: Okay, here is your spoon. See I'm putting it in the jar. (pause)
Baby: (Giggles)
Mom: Ohhh, delicious oatmeal. Here it comes! (pause)
Baby: Ba.

Of a multitude of such moments is an English-speaker born. So if you're not the one at home with your baby, make sure who ever is, or whichever day-care center you use, understands the importance of conversing with your child. When you're home, yammer away while you're emptying the dishwasher, sing while you're pushing the stroller. Chat while chewing on bagels. Focus your conversation on what interests baby, which will inevitably be what's right in front of his or her face ("see the red ball!") or what he or she is feeling ("you're crying because you're sad") and not the current price of internet stocks. When your child begins to use language to communicate, respond with wild enthusiasm. When he points and says "dat" or just grunts at the banana on top of the refrigerator, give it to him. That's how he'll learn there's power in words. (A lesson you'll one day regret, at which point turn to "Don't Take It Personally," on p.148).

But Don't Depend on Words

Yes, babies are sponges for language. But don't rely on "No!" if your child is about to stick a wee finger into an outlet or knock over a lit candlestick. Pick him up and move him away. Tell him it's not safe, of course, but don't expect words to be enough. Babies often don't understand verbal warnings and commands no matter how booming, threatening or scared your tone of voice. It's not fun to have to rouse yourself from that plush armchair you've finally plopped into—but that's the only way to guarantee she doesn't pull down the drapes.

Even if danger isn't quite so imminent, you're better off responding to your child's behavior with your hands along with your mouth. If you just sit back and say "No!" "No!" NO!" increasing your volume as she increases the TV volume two things will occur. The first is that your child will be on the receiving end of a lot of shouted "NOs" which is a hurtful thing for her to hear from you all day long. The second is that she'll probably keep on doing what she's doing anyway—not out of spite or even daring necessarily, but simply because she's a baby and there's a whole lot she just doesn't "get" yet.

At this age you also can't rely on words to encourage proper social behavior. A two-year-old can be issued a reminder to share when the grabbies set in. She may not want to comply, but she'll hear and understand your words. But at a year or eighteen months, your grand parental announcement, "no grabbing" is not likely to faze her or even register. You need to *show* rather than just tell her how to take turns with the ball.

Certainly you should continue to talk to very young children about what they should and shouldn't do. The route to learning language is to hear it used over and over again in situations that are pertinent to you. She won't understand "no grabbing" the first time. But by the thirtieth or one-hundredth time she will. You want her to grow up in a verbally rich world, since this will help her communicate better throughout life. So keep talking. Eventually most young children are able to process verbal commands to a sophisticated enough degree that they can respond to them quickly (if they want). But until then, don't *just* say "No!"

Use a Playpen

Of course you're delighted that your child can finally crawl. Becoming mobile is one of those crucial first steps toward independence. Still, you're horrified to discover that what she's crawling toward is your Tiffany lamp—a family heirloom that's about to become ten pounds of shattered glass. You will hear again and again that conscientious child-proofing is the solution to the demolition derby that a crawling baby brings into your home. Certainly, nothing is more important than making sure that such perils as hot stoves, electric outlets and cleaning fluids are unreachable. But you will also hear that once you've done this childproofing you should let your little one scoot about freely, all the time, any time. Otherwise, some experts warn, your child's intellectual and motor growth may be stifled.

But even in a completely child-proofed environment, little kids have a talent for courting catastrophe. No matter how many locks you have on your kitchen cabinets, children this age attach themselves to trouble as readily as Velcro. Which means they still have to be watched constantly—especially if they're on the active side. This wouldn't be a problem if you never wanted to take fifteen minutes to drink some java and read the paper, or make a phone call or finally go to the bathroom. The solution: use a playpen and *don't feel guilty*.

Too many enlightened parents consider playpens anathema—hideous holdovers from the Dark Ages of parenting when Mom would put the playpen in front of the TV and let Captain Kangaroo keep baby company while she ironed down in the basement. Not the best approach to brain development.

I suspect that playpens waned in popularity at around the same time that so many progressive zoos did away with cages. I think it's great that the gorillas in the midst of the Bronx zoo get to roam in a simulacrum of an African rainforest. But if your natural habitat is not the Congo but a room with pastel bunnies stenciled on the wall, there's nothing cruel about being penned in now and then.

Twenty minutes behind mesh is not going to ruin your child's development. It's not going to stymie creativity, exploration or independence. It's just going to mean that you get to brush your teeth without feeling like a stopwatch is ticking.

There are sacrifices we make for children that make good sense—working less, reading *Pat the Bunny* instead of the paper, forgoing vacations in order to save for college, etc. If you have young children you owe them nothing less than to put their needs first, even when that's inconvenient. But as in all things, you can carry this to ridiculous extremes. Dissing playpens falls into this category.

So instead of banning the playpen, just use it responsibly. Get a big one (not one of those now-popular folding, cushiony cribs that double as travel playpens) and use it before your child becomes a crawler so that she's used to it. Stick it someplace visually interesting, preferably in full view of you and whatever it is you're doing. Be sure you put a bunch of special, tempting toys in there with her. If she wants out, try distraction and all the other typical tricks. No success? Let her out—it's a playpen not a prison. In such a case, use the playpen only for emergencies, like when the cat fertilizes your carpet or a glass bowl shatters. Even if she's having a ball try not to keep her in there for more than twenty minutes or so. Never deposit her in there for a time-out—you want her to have happy associations with the playpen.

Most children come to accept and even enjoy being in a playpen—at least until they're walking. If yours falls into this category, feel happy not guilty. Any baby would tell you she'd rather spend some time being fenced in if in return she gets a happy, rested parent instead of a zombie.

Distract Them

Children are born willful. That's because they need gumption to do the hard work of learning to roll over, sit, crawl, stand, walk and reprogram your VCR. But some days their single-mindedness can be exasperating. What do you do when he stiffens like a board when you need to put him in the stroller? Or screams in his high chair because he can't reach that bright shiny toy, otherwise known as your meat cleaver? Of all the wondrous qualities possessed by the typical infant, there are times when the one you'll be most grateful for is his spotty short-term memory. By honing the fine art of distraction there will be many occasions when you'll be able to spare his tears— and your ears. Try the following techniques. The more of them you use at the same time, the higher your success rate is likely to be.

Relocate him.
Once your baby is taken out of his high chair and placed on his bedroom floor with his Pooh bear and bunny blocks, the cleaver may quickly fade into distant memory. Five minutes can be light years for children this age.

Turn on some music.
Few kids can resist it. Get him clapping his hands and "singing" along. Meanwhile, the cleaver disappears into a drawer.

Feed him.

You don't want to play this hand too often since it's probably not wise to program kids to use food for comfort. But on a good day you can short-circuit a major meltdown with the kindly offer of a cracker.

Get all excited.

It doesn't matter what you're getting all enthusiastic about. But if you smile, open your eyes wide and say, "Oh! Look! A . . . a . . . Birdie! Outside the window! Ooooo! See the birdie?" you can easily guide him into his stroller while he's searching the sky. Keep up the patter: "Oh, such a nice birdie! Tweet tweet it says," while you strap him in.

Wait two minutes.

If your attempt to change a diaper is resisted, be patient. Instead of trying to wrestle, let her spend some time looking at a book or a rattle, or singing a song. Give it about 120 seconds and most likely she'll forget that she's in the middle of a diaper strike. Then, without announcing it, simply get to work on her bottom.

These techniques are not foolproof. If they work this time, they won't necessarily work the next. And eventually, as your children grow, you will be astounded by their memory. Instead of distracting them you will have to move on to the more complex parental arts, namely: bribery, blackmail and keeping cleavers under lock and key.

Don't Fear Their Tears

It's normal for babies to cry—a lot. Not every tear signals a true emergency or heartbreak requiring mega-doses of TLC. Yes, you should always comfort a crying infant. But little kids—especially those who can't yet talk well—will cry over minor incidents that are far from frightful to them, because they don't really have any other way to communicate that they are upset. Rushing over with open arms and a look of sympathetic horror every time your baby falls on her Pampered bottom or can't maneuver the square peg into the right hole will convince her that she really *should* be traumatized by such trivia. We all know people who grow up believing that, and they are as annoying as all hell.

In some cases, the best policy is to ignore the cries. This works well if your child becomes frustrated while trying to master some skill that she's on the verge of "getting"—like bringing the spoon to her mouth or walking without holding on. If you wait a moment the crisis is likely to pass, replaced by the sheer joy of having done it herself—or the distraction of noticing your car keys on the shelf.

Don't Expect to "Snooze When the Baby Does"

This is one of the worst frauds perpetrated against new parents. You will hear it countless times: The best way to avoid sleep deprivation is to nod off when your baby falls asleep. But some babies just don't sleep. Others doze for an hour or so. By the time you're ready to do the same, the baby is spitting up. You're lucky if you get in one baby-sized nap a day. You are more likely to find yourself spending baby's down time doing everything else your continued existence requires, like paying bills and, oh yes, eating. Even if you accept as much help as you can humanly beg or pay for, you will probably still be exhausted. It's in the best interest of your own sanity and your loving relationships with other adults to acknowledge that the birth of a baby is a time of crisis. It's a joyful time, but it is an utterly exhausting one. Until your newborn figures out the difference between night and day there won't be much difference between the two for you either.

TODDLERS

Don't Ask, Tell

Michael got tired of walking around the toy store, so he did what many a typical two-year-old would do. He flung the little boxes of Slinkys off the shelves, then tried to total the dump truck display with a plastic bat. Enter, Mom, her voice dripping with diplomacy: "OK, Michael. Would you like to get into your stroller now?"

"No!" said Michael.

"Well I think it's time to go home and nap, don't you?" implored Mom. This, of course, produced a tantrum of Hollywood proportions. Finally the poor woman wised up, picked him up, plunked him in the stroller and rolled him out of the mall. (He was asleep before she got to her car.)

Being a parent would be far less challenging if all it took was giving gentle *suggestions* to children rather than handing out direct orders. After all, every sensitive parent remembers how oppressive it felt to have your elders bark commands at you. Once your child reaches adolescence, direct orders aren't likely to get you far. But for the diaper set they're *de rigeur*. Yes, you want to teach your child to make his own choices (see p. 39). But there are times when the best motto is (to borrow one of my dad's favorite cornballs): "When I want your opinion I'll give it to you." You don't ever have to come on like a drill sergeant. But don't give your toddler a say if there's only one "right" answer.

If there's no time to spare and your child won't get into the stroller, exit the playground, or put down the electric cord you need to gently but firmly force him to do what you need him to, whether that means you lift him up or force dangerous objects out of his grip. Just a firm but pleasant (if you can manage it) "Time to go" is all you need say. You're the parent, he's the child. You make the rules. And that's the way it is.

Not only does being authoritarian when necessary make life run more smoothly—and safely—it also prevents you from overburdening a tot with decision-making she's not really ready to handle. No self-respecting two-year-old will willingly get back into the stroller when fatigue strikes at the playground. She's more apt to get hyper—to try to climb up that slide one more time even if that means she's going to tumble off. She's not old enough to know what's good for her—so you have to make choices for her.

Asking her a loaded question isn't just unfair and manipulative, it's more likely to make her uncooperative. If your child is feeling disagreeable (and, let's face, at this age it's their *job* to feel that way) all you get for your diplomacy is a major power struggle. To borrow a cornball from my mother: A family is not always a democracy. If you don't want your child to have a choice in the matter, don't give her a vote.

When It Gets Too Quiet, Worry

One morning eighteen-month-old Brad reached up higher than he ever had before and grabbed the huge jar of petroleum jelly off his bedroom shelf. He then proceeded to finger-paint his entire body, his toddler bed and the walls. Where was his mother while all of this was happening? In the kitchen, reading a six-month-old issue of a parenting magazine and congratulating herself, since it was clearly due to her superior mothering skills that Brad was finally learning to play independently in his bedroom. Being a first-time mother, she didn't realize that silence on the part of a young child should set off sirens in your head louder than a KISS reunion concert. You are surely headed for a disaster. With luck, it will only be of gigantic, rather than tragic, proportions—just a truly annoying, time-consuming disaster which you will only finally find humorous when . . . well, maybe never. If a non-sleeping child aged three or under is alone and quiet for more than ninety seconds, run like hell. You may get there in time.

Respect Their Rituals

When the world seems like a big and complicated place it helps a child to be able to think, "this much, at least, I know for sure." It's a relief that Mommy will always greet him with a good morning hug and say, "hello honey bunny." He has learned to expect that his baby-sitter doesn't come until *after* Daddy leaves for work. At nursery school he knows that there's always a story after they play outside, and that they will sing "Tingalayo" before dismissal. Because children's minds are so bright and fluid and, yes, chaotic, these certainties help to anchor them, to prevent the feeling that the world is crowding in and overwhelming them.

Most kids this age take comfort in the routines of their lives. But some seem to take the need for routines very far. They get out of sorts if you so much as cut their turkey sandwich into rectangles rather than triangles or put on both their socks before putting on their left shoe. Suddenly you find yourself taking orders over ridiculous minutiae from a two-year-old tyrant. It takes a lot of patience to cope with a child who dissolves or erupts when you put her oatmeal in her Barney bowl because the one with the fairy is dirty—considering how much else you have to do at the moment it hardly seems a priority to wash the bowl out. Shouldn't a two-year-old learn flexibility and patience anyway?

Yes and no. If your child is rigid about rituals the best approach is to go along with them as much as you can. Your child has devised rituals because she needs them. They don't signal a future obsessive-compulsive disorder. They are a sign that she's trying to instill some control over her environment (which includes you) and herself. Expect that her demands in this area may become greater in times of stress—such as when she's sick or you move or she's starting a new school.

At the same time, try to prevent your child from adding new rituals. Otherwise, the bedtime shtick that started with a story and a kiss goodnight can turn into an intricate, multi-step procedure entailing proscribed numbers of hugs, kisses, drinks of water and whatnot. Since the basis of this need for rituals is to alleviate anxiety, it isn't going to do your child much good if you attempt to go along with endless rituals that drive you nuts, and leave you feeling angry and distant. Better to be firm about your own limits.

If you feel frustration brewing because your child is demanding in this area, you may be rightly perceiving that at the heart of her urgent request for another glass of water is a power play. Her real need may be to control you rather than to quench her thirst. You can't blame her for trying, considering how little in control of you she really is. But you also can't let her get away with it. Nobody benefits if you rock your four-year-old to sleep every night after reading *Goodnight Moon* three times and offering up the required two cups of water in her favorite yellow cup.

Try to get her to talk about her wishes and desire for more power, rather than act it out in manipulative ways. If she's tearful because you refuse to comply with her third post tuck-in request—which is for you to bring up her ballet slippers from the basement—acknowledge how much she must wish that you would always do exactly what she wants. Muse out loud about how much she probably wishes she made the rules. During the day, encourage (but don't force) her to play table-turning games in which she's the parent and you—or a dolly, teddy or action figure—are the kid. Ask her what rules she would make up if she were in charge. The more you let her see that it's okay to be up-front about such wishes, the less likely that she'll try to manipulate you covertly by, say, refusing to give you your car keys when you're late for work. Remember, too, that driving you crazy may be part of the pleasure in the rituals for her. In such cases, the more seemingly patient you are the shorter these rites are likely to be.

Count to Three

With an astoundingly high frequency rate, toddlers will stop whatever dangerous or annoying antic they are in the midst of and become immediately compliant if you announce that you're about to count to three. My guess is that this is simply an early manifestation of that inborn human trait—hatred of deadlines. Plus, they can't stand it when you set a time limit on their personal power. They know that if they don't get into the stroller or out of the car seat by "three" they will have to bear the insult of being repositioned by you. My theories may be wrong. We may never know why "I'm going to count to three" are some of the real magic words of parenting. But who cares? What matters is that they work so often.

If you are fortunate enough to have a child who jumps when you count, be careful not to squander this power. To avoid diluting the technique's effectiveness:

Don't wimp out.

If your child doesn't comply by "three" carry through on the promised consequences. This means thinking ahead before you announce a countdown. Are you really going to throw the stuffed Barney out the window? Or do a turnaround at the airport and *not* go to Uncle Jeff's for Thanksgiving? If you're not, don't say you are—otherwise one of two unfortunate events will result. Either your child will call your bluff, see the humbug behind the curtain and never again hup to it when you start counting. Or, in fear that this will happen, you will find yourself stopping the count altogether—which sends another message of weakness, and kids even this young can tell when you're on the verge of wimping out. So if you find yourself sending up a little prayer before uttering "three" your threats are too big. Make sure they are dramatic enough to motivate your child, but small enough that you're willing to follow through.

Don't overuse it.

Employ counting only as a last resort, after the failure of all of your far more creative attempts to get her to brush her teeth, like chasing her into the bathroom as if you're the tooth fairy. If you're responding to every act of sudden deafness on your child's part by threatening to count, you're using this tactic too much. Limit yourself to one count a day or better yet about three counts a week.

Don't teach fourth-grade math when he's only three.

Too many children become early whizzes at fractions. They know that before Mom gets to "three" a cozy cushion of time will be taken up with 2 1/4, 2 1/2, 2 3/4. In some families, the count even gets divided into eighths. Go ahead, tell yourself that you're just trying to improve our nation's abysmal math scores. This is a noble public service that will no doubt help to save us from economic collapse in 2020, but what you're really doing is stalling. If your child typically needs more time to comply, count to five or ten, but leave fractions out of it. Kids learn soon enough that if you're threatening them with fourths (even if your voice becomes sterner and higher pitched with each fractional increase), you're afraid to carry through on your threat. Which from their perspective means there's a good chance that you probably won't.

Sing It

"Okay, let's get on your shoes, time to go home!" You're being cheerful and reasonable and what do you get as your reward? A red Mary Jane hurled vaguely in your direction and an emphatic, "No, I'm *not*." Want to breathe deeply and start over?

This time try *singing*. This secret weapon works for a reason only the pied piper knew for sure. Little kids love music, so maybe singing an order works because they focus on the melody and get distracted from being ornery. Or perhaps music is so associated with pleasantness and playtime that putting on shoes and saying bye-bye to the beat becomes a game.

Whatever the cause, what's important is that singing is so effective with many two- and three-year-olds. If you keep up the cheerfulness, but add "It's time to put on your shoooooeees," in any sing-song melody of your choice you dramatically up the odds that your child will comply. Keep in mind, though, that this is a *preventive* technique. If you're already fending off flying leather it's probably too late to strike up a tune.

Use the Other Magic Word: Special

Of all the explanations for the typical toddler's relatively minute attention span, the one I like best is that he is so eager to learn about the world that he doesn't have time to linger. Once he's explored something he's on to the next challenge. New experiences are a young child's brain-food, which helps explain his "been there, done that" attitude toward the talking Arthur doll that captivated him yesterday. It's this tendency that explains why the word "special" is one of a harried parent's secret weapons. A two-year-old who turns up her nose at a glass of orange juice might gulp it down enthusiastically if she's told it comes from Grandma's special supermarket or is being poured for her into a special cup. To little ones, "special" resonates with all things exceptional and wonderful—like their birthday or Christmas. Throwing the adjective in before anything is no guarantee. But if you're lucky, even the antibiotic prescribed for her ear-infection will get gulped down if you mix it with some punch and call it "special juice."

Hover

Perhaps your toddler is like this: You don't have to hold her hand when you walk down the street because she would never suddenly dart into traffic. A porcelain piggy bank sits unscathed on a low windowsill in her bedroom. She has never pulled on an electrical cord, tried to open a kitchen cabinet, pushed a button because it was there. If your toddler can be let loose in a hardware store, the only thing you really need to check is that you're remembering her birth date correctly.

But for those of us whose toddlers act their age, constant vigilance is required. Let's face it, there's a fair amount of drudgery in caring for children who think more with their fingers and feet than their heads. Say you go toddler-in-tow to a dinner party at a friend's apartment. The parents of the four- and five-year-olds sit around sipping their cups and sampling coffee cake. All of their children are ensconced in the playroom with Barbie and the talking Chuckie doll. Your twenty-month-old, however, will not sit still, so neither can you. During the moment you take to pour yourself some coffee he's waddled into the kitchen and turned on the dishwasher. By the time you get there, he's found the knife drawer. The front door is opened for a late arrival and he darts out and into the elevator just before the door closes.

Rest assured that by the time he's ready for kindergarten you will have plenty of such stories to tell. The key, of course, is to make sure they all have happy endings. The only way to do that is to stay on top of him. If you have a toddler who's theme song is, "I'm a Wanderer" then yours ought to be, "I'm a Hoverer."

Hovering means that you are on constant alert while watching your child. It doesn't mean that you put your *child* on constant alert by yelling "careful!" at her at thirty-second intervals. If you're a nervous hoverer you risk squelching her adventurous spirit (See "Don't Overreact," p. 50) which you don't want to do. You just want to keep her safe.

Part of hovering is to anticipate the unexpected. If your child is in a situation where she could theoretically hurt herself severely you have to take precautions as if it's a foregone conclusion that otherwise she will. Frankly, I think you need to do this even if you do have the rare toddler who is hardware-store friendly. And, even if you cannot conceive of her suddenly attempting a quick dash into oncoming traffic you should still hold her hand tightly when you walk down the street. Ask any emergency room doctor and he or she will tell you it's a constant refrain. A child is injured and the parent says, "But she never tried to climb out the window before."

When it comes to toddler exploits there is always a first time because children make sudden, unexpected developmental leaps. These can prove harmful if their parents haven't fully anticipated them. Maxine learned this the hard way one day while she was telling her sister over the phone how relieved she felt now that Lucas was a year old. His sleep problems seemed to be behind him, and since he couldn't walk yet, she didn't have to watch him like a hawk. She felt she was finally getting back a little bit of her old life. Right on cue she heard a crash and a wail from the living room where Lucas had been playing with his stuffed animals. She found him sprawled on the floor amid shards of broken pottery. He had piled three of his teddy bears on a chair and climbed up to grab a bud from a vase. Lucas was fine but Maxine wasn't. Once her heart rate returned to normal she made a vow to be a hoverer.

Every child's early years are filled with firsts. But there are some firsts you never want your kids to get to. The only way to avoid them is to be on the lookout. Always.

Sit on Your Hands

When your children are little you can't take hovering too far. But hovering wisely also means knowing when *not* to intervene.

Since kids learn from experience you want to make sure that your vigilance doesn't prevent them from exploring and satisfying their curiosity. Avoid letting your concern for their safety spill over into an overriding assumption that they are helpless. When her chubby little hands shove you away because she wants to cross the street herself, you don't let go. But when those same hands want to snap her cardigan let her try even if she can't yet do it herself. Await an invitation before you help her. If you are programmed to aid your child in every way, you'll need to control that impulse. Sometimes the best thing you can do for your child is literally to sit on your hands.

It may be the biggest of parenthood's many challenges that after you have thoroughly learned a response, you suddenly have to unlearn it in a hurry. You are so used to turning on the light switch for your son that you do it automatically. But as soon as he can reach it, he will cry bitterly if you flick it before he does. Same goes for pouring his cereal, squeezing the toothpaste onto his toothbrush, Velcro-ing his shoes. It is hard to keep pace with children. You will always be one step behind in your assumptions about their abilities. This is a fact of parenting. Offer your child your humble apologies and next time try to remember she can reboot the computer herself.

When your child becomes older, sitting on your hands will become metaphorical. It will mean not nagging about his homework or his girlfriend. It will mean letting him think and act for himself, and cope with the consequences of his decisions. As difficult as sitting on your hands may be now, you might as well get used to it. Someday he'll have a driver's license.

PRESCHOOLERS

Don't Expect an Easy "Threes"

Where did this damaging misinformation come from? So many parents have come to expect that sandwiched between the "terrible" twos and "beyond terrible" fours will be the breezy threes—a twelve-month respite during which your child is suddenly rational enough not to bang his head on the sidewalk because you won't allow him to drive the Camaro and blasé enough not to care if he doesn't get to do everything first. Don't believe it. Every age and stage of childhood has its charms and its challenges and three is no different. Yes, some children do become more agreeable around their third birthday. But some become newly "terrible."

The irony is that parents have been so forewarned about the terrible twos that they await with dread the transformation of their darling infant into an impossible toddler. But sometimes the twos are delightful, which leaves the parents thinking they are home free. And then, around the third birthday, the tantrums, the orneriness, the penchant for throwing food finally arrive. The worst of it is that compared with a two-year-old, a three-year-old has far more endurance and lung power, as well as better aim.

There are some textbook differences between your standard two-year-old and three-year-old. At three a child is better able to separate from his mother. He is more aware of—and more interested in—the world outside his home.

But sometimes this ability to separate gets exaggerated in parents' minds. Many experts claim that "three" is the perfect age for becoming an older sibling, since you're mature enough not to need your mommy constantly like a baby does, but young enough to grow up feeling a connection with your new brother or sister. But countless parents who spaced their children "by the book" will tell you that their three-year-old wasn't as ready as they had hoped to handle big sisterhood. Sometimes, having kids three years apart is a recipe for the most intense sibling rivalry. I'm not making categorical recommendations for the spacing of children, but simply forewarning you not to expect too much from three-year-olds. They may indeed be potty trained and able to form multi-word sentences. Many of them can happily wave good-bye to Mommy or Daddy and join their nursery school class without feeling unbearably homesick. But they are very new at being pre-schoolers. Subject them to stress and more often they react like toddlers, not like the bigger kids they are growing into bit by bit. So accept their limitations. Base your expectations on what *your* child can handle, not on what some textbook says she should be ready for.

Stop the Endless Negotiating

If you've been raising your child to delight in making her own decisions, by now you probably have a highly opinionated preschooler. This is good—up to a point. You'll know you've reached that point if your child is ready to conclude that *everything* is negotiable. You tell him he may have one piece of his Halloween candy—either a lollipop or a marshmallow. "Four!" he counters—holding up two lollipops and two marshmallows. You say only two. He holds out for three. You give in. Then he announces that, since the marshmallow is so small, it's really okay for him to have another one, right?

Congratulations. Your child has begun to master one of the hallmarks of civilization—the fine art of haggling. In the long run this is not a bad thing. By the time he is grown, you want him to be an expert in gracefully getting what he wants—or at least what he can live with—from you, his teachers, friends, and future loved ones, not to mention all of those "customer service representatives." You can't teach him this skill if you're unilateral in your dealings with him. "My way or no way" pretty much sums up the typical four-year-old's approach to life. But it is not the motto of a discerning parent. For children to grow, you have to let them make choices. Over time, they are supposed to gradually erode your power base.

You know all of this, which is why you respond with a chuckle of pride when Celeste starts to use her smarts to get more out of you than you were prepared to give. But soon things are getting out of hand. Little Celeste seems to be in training for a career in arbitration. She wants to dicker over what time you'll be home from work, how much TV she can watch, when to leave the playground, etc.

If your days are punctuated by your child's wrangling with you over everything from what to wear to which book to read first, one of two things is true. Either you're a softy who gives in to her so much that she's losing respect for your rules—or you're a hard-ass with too many trivial rules to begin with. In either case, the way to move the power gauge between parent and child back to its rightful setting (in which you have most, but she gets enough) is to *stop negotiating*.

If you're a softy, frequent negotiations are just sapping you of too much parental power. You may have lost sight of the fact that a child's longing to take charge of her own destiny has to be tempered with some parental backbone. It is all too easy to give children more power and control than they are ready to exercise. If you yourself find it difficult to bend to authority you may identify with your child's plight and unwittingly indulge her. But it won't benefit your child if she ends up with more candy than she can stomach, and less sleep than she really needs. If you are giving in too much, remind yourself that you really know what's better for your child. Don't worry that doing things your way will permanently damage her fragile little ego. More harm will come if she grows up like Yertle the Turtle, believing she's the ruler of all she can see.

On the other hand, if you're a hard ass you're forcing your child to bargain with you over requests you should simply say yes to. You'll know this is true if you find yourself drawn into ridiculous arguments with your four-year-old over whether she will wear the pajamas she took out of her drawer or the ones you chose for her. Remember that in order to remain powerful in your child's eyes, you don't have to make her feel power*less*. Try to follow her lead with a smile when it comes to *trivial* requests, like whether she can watch *Sesame Street* and then have breakfast. If there's time, why not? Give her some room to flex her fledgling negotiating muscles. If you're not sure how you feel about your child's request you don't have to give an immediate answer. You can say, "Let me think about it," rather than "no."

Sometimes parents become overly strict because deep down they fear that otherwise they won't be able to control their child. It can feel threatening to your authority when your child begins to use verbal slight-of-hand to gain an advantage. You'll find it easier to remain inwardly amused by her shrewdness if you remember that her tendency to challenge is both normal and wonderful. True, her delivery and approach may need some refining. But when she announces at the top of her lungs that she hates green food and is never going to eat dinner again if a string bean comes within smelling distance of her plate, she is asserting her selfhood. She is developing a sense of who she is and what she wants, prefers, even *demands.* I'm not saying you should tolerate airborne string beans or yelling at the dinner table. But educating her so she can more gracefully get what she needs from you (and life in general) is not the same as trying to eradicate this natural urge to be in control.

Not all parents are classic softies or hard-asses. Many of us fluctuate between these two extremes. We get disgusted with ourselves for lazily indulging our children, so we suddenly come down hard on a reasonable request—like getting to play a few extra minutes in the tub—that we otherwise would readily agree to. Or, we worry that we've been coming down too hard lately so we bend over backwards to be accommodating—in the form of allowing apple pie to serve as breakfast food or buying some ridiculous toy.

Somewhere between being a softy and a hard-ass lies the royal road to perfect parenting. Whichever side of the road you're on, you can pitch yourself closer to the center by remembering that not everything is—or should have to be—negotiable.

Don't Offer False Praise

Maggie's gymnastic class is performing for their parents. She and two other little girls are supposed to demonstrate, one at a time, how to do a forward roll. The first two accomplish this feat with ease. But Maggie's forward flip is a flop. She tries it again and does worse. The audience of adults still cheers heartily, of course. Her dad, John, sits with his heart in his throat. He knows Maggie has worked very hard on her forward roll and was very excited about showing off what she had learned. He fears his daughter's fledgling ego has been bruised by her, dare we say, failure. When the show is over, John rushes up to Maggie and says, "You were great!" exuding just as much enthusiasm and delight as when Maggie learned to spell her name—which was a real accomplishment.

The catch, of course, is that Maggie didn't do well on any level. She didn't do as well as the other girls, but far more importantly she didn't do as well as she had expected to. It's hard to blame her dad for mustering up some praise. Who wouldn't want to erase a child's chagrin and disappointment? Especially these days when we're told again and again that bolstering a child's self-esteem is crucial for everything from optimizing their grade point average to preventing a life of drug abuse.

The problem is that praising a child undeservedly is more damaging to the child than is the failure itself. Sure, self-esteem can be an asset, but only if it is reality-based. If you grow up with a sense of self-congratulation that is not supported by any actual accomplishments, self-esteem can be a major liability. We all know people who think they are better than they really are. Not only are they roundly disliked, but it is *harder* for them to achieve their potential than others whose self-worth is spiked with a dollop of self-doubt. Raise your children on a diet of empty praise and they'll have a harder time accomplishing the greatness within them.

Yes, it is imperative to give children the constant message that they are beloved by you, unconditionally and forever. But that's not the same as telling them that everything they do is top drawer. If John defines all of Maggie's attempts as "wonderful" Maggie may come to believe it. This prevents her father from succeeding at one of a parent's most important jobs—teaching your child to learn from her mistakes. On the other hand, if Maggie is savvy enough to see through Dad's false praise, she may end up discounting *all* the kudos Dad throws her way—including the ones she's really earned. So much for teaching self-esteem!

I'm hardly suggesting that you be critical of your children. You can damage a young child if you tend to point out to her where she falls short when compared with others. Children shouldn't be made to feel that they haven't accomplished if they can't ride their trike as well as Tommy or finger-paint as creatively as Bessie. They should be measured against themselves and praised when they make progress. Even when a child "fails" you can still praise her—not for her accomplishment, but for how hard she tried or how well she's handling her disappointment.

John really didn't need to use praise as a psychological Band-Aid. He would have helped his daughter more if he was warm and supportive without pretending that everything was okay. He could have approached Maggie in a way that left his daughter comfortable expressing any sadness she was feeling—without assuming or implying that Maggie was sad at all. (She might be feeling just fine about her flop.) John could have said something like, "So how did it feel being on stage?" or "What did you think of your forward roll?" He could have told Maggie how much he enjoyed watching her. And then, if Maggie expressed disappointment or anger over her mistake, he could have helped her grapple with those feelings. He could have reminded her of how hard she tried and that if she practiced even more next time she'd probably do much better. Taking this approach will help Maggie achieve more. The end result will be that at Maggie's next recital both she and Dad will be genuinely beaming when she finally does a forward roll worth flipping over.

Let Them Win

Until about age four most children are pretty much oblivious to competition. They care little about being the best, the winner or the leader. Their lives revolve around themselves and the grownups who love them. And then suddenly they begin to notice the world out there. As their bodies and minds become stronger and more agile they revel in their growing strength, savvy and independence. Once they recognize what a great thing it is to be able to control your life (and other people, too) they naturally become obsessed with power—wanting as much of it as they can get. In fact, they want all of it. And because at four wishing makes it so, they assume they are indeed all-powerful. There are few creatures on earth more grandiose than a typical four-year-old. He both takes for granted that he is at the center of the universe, and deeply fears that this may not be the case. The result is that he may crumble and/or get extremely argumentative when fate intervenes with the announcement that somebody else won at Candyland, or big brother gets to climb into the car first today.

The natural tendency when your child starts acting this way is to lecture him or her: don't cheat, don't be a sore loser, wait your turn. It's certainly reasonable to offer up these pearls of wisdom—just don't expect your child to accept them, yet. A four-year-old who only wants to play if he is declared the winner before the game even starts will not necessarily be devoid of scruples as an adult—or even as a six-year-old.

As necessary as it is to teach a young child good values, you also need to accept his overriding need to believe in his own super powers. When his longing to be number one infringes on other's rights (when, for example, he cheats against a friend while playing Chutes and Ladders) you do need to set him straight about the rules—and even suggest the game not commence if you know he's not yet capable of being a gracious loser (or winner).

But in the comfort of his own home, you can relax the rules. As difficult as it is for a young child to lose against a friend, it may be excruciating for him to lose against a parent. The tantrum that ensues if Mom gets to King Candy first is fueled by a deep sense of betrayal. So, either put the game away or let him win. If he wants to race you up the stairs or down the block, go as slowly as it takes to make sure he is victorious. Likewise, if he tells you he's the best, fastest, smartest, tallest, and most adorable kid in his class/day-care center or street don't argue with him. Just listen good-naturedly. To point out his flaws or suggest he get a more realistic perspective of his place in the pecking order will just anger or shatter him.

At the same time, of course, you should clue him in to the rules of the real world. Let him know it's okay to peek at and even reshuffle the cards when he's playing against you (at four. As he gets older you don't need to allow this). But if he gets creative with the rules when playing against a friend it's called cheating and isn't permitted. You should also point out that his friends long to be number one just as much as he does, so everyone needs to get a chance to be first.

Don't worry that if you indulge him at home he'll never learn sportsmanship. He'll have plenty of opportunity in the years ahead to prove you wrong. But by indulging him now you'll give him something else that will benefit him for a lifetime. Most of us have within us a little voice that revs us up when we're feeling down. When the going looks tough that little voice holds out with the deep conviction that somehow we can prevail. It is often what helps us to accomplish our full potential. That voice is the vestige of our four-year-old self. So if you want your child's future to be triumphant, don't silence that voice now. Let him crow.

Teach Them Your Values

When children begin day-care or preschool their ears, noses, throats, and stomachs are assaulted by cold and flu viruses. But when they begin to have drop-off playdates (usually at age four or five) they may fall prey to a far worse affliction than sniffles and stomach flus. I call it the family values virus. At Bradley's house your son learns the term "butt head." Your daughter nonchalantly dumps her dinner in the sink, since Abby's mother lets *her* waste food. You don't allow toy guns, Eric's garage is full of them. You're Jewish, but Lauren's parents spend every Sunday morning in church so now your daughter wants to go too.

This problem doesn't come up if the other child's family is seriously dysfunctional. In that case you just avoid playdates and thank the stars that your child is still young enough for you to pick his friends. But what if there's nothing technically wrong with the other family—their worldview is just different from yours? You might as well figure out what to do about this now because you will be confronting challenges to your values throughout childhood and in spades once adolescence hits. The best defense is a strong offense. Start by deciding for yourself if the friendship is important for your child. It's worth putting up with a few extra helpings of gum drops added to her diet or an occasional car-chase heavy TV show if the other child is a good friend. When that's the case, make sure you're countering your child's new exposure to the world with deeper exposure to your perspective. Don't put the other family down, just make it clear that in your home french fries are not considered vegetables and weekly jaunts to the toy store are not on the schedule. Tell her it's fine for Abby's mommy to make the rules for Abby and that it's interesting to see how other families do things, but that doesn't change the rules at your home. This approach works for the wide range of contrasts your child is likely to note, from differences in religion to variations in consumption of saturated fat.

In measured doses these experiences can build character. Keep kids sheltered and someday when you aren't there to make choices for them, they may get drenched. Letting them see how other families live helps them find their place in the world.

Have Great Expectations

Your daughter is fumbling with her zipper. "I can't do it!" she whines, emphasizing each word with a total-body shake. You should say:

A) "Stop that whining! Don't be such a baby!"
B) "I see you're getting frustrated. That's a tough zipper."
C) "Okay, calm down. Here, let me help you."
D) "Yes you can! Keep trying, you'll do it."

Obviously we can rule out A. But the other three are all respectful, loving choices. Which one is best? It's fine to empathize with a child when she's feeling frustrated (B), and there are times when the most expedient approach may be to help her (C), but the best outcome of the zipper episode is for her to learn she can work through something hard and *succeed,* which is why D is the best choice.

Sometimes parents worry so much about putting undo pressure on a child that they forget the importance of instilling self-confidence. If a child feels like giving up she's much better off getting a pep talk than just having her feelings of frustration validated and/or having you rescue her. Since they are human, children will inevitably try to whine or squirm their way out of doing things they think are boring or difficult. If your child often expresses this attitude then a good attitude to express back is, "Mommys (or Daddies) help children who help themselves."

This policy only works if you have a clear idea of what your child is and isn't capable of. If you overestimate your child you may end up being too tough on him, demanding he accomplish feats he's not developmentally ready for. But far more often parents underestimate their kids. And since children tend to rise to your level of expectation, the more you underestimate them, the less they are able to do for themselves.

It's hard *not* to underestimate kids because they all grow at warp speed. One day it's a struggle for her to draw a square, you turn around and she's writing her full name on every blank piece of paper she can find. One day he can't get his thumb around his shirt snap—a week goes by and he can do it in ten seconds flat.

One sign that you are downplaying your child's abilities is if he seems to be at very different stages at home and away from you. You are amazed when the preschool teacher tells you he goes to the toilet unaided—at home you are still the official pants puller-downer. You gape as he cooperatively takes part in the class cleanup, enthusiastically wiping the table. It never occurred to you that he might be ready to take on some chores at home. You watch cringing as your son climbs onto the monkey bars and attempts to swing across the overhead ladder. To your amazement he does it. Last summer he couldn't. But that was then and this, for one fleeting moment, is now.

Perhaps he has made these advances while away from home not because he has been pressured, but because his teacher or baby-sitter assumed he could do it—and so he did. Try it at home. Tell him that even if something is hard it's worth attempting. The more he does it the easier it will be. When he fails be optimistic ("next time will be better") and supportive ("you should be proud of yourself for trying so hard.") At all costs, avoid motivating him through criticism (see p.172). There's a big difference between saying, "I know that soon you will be ready to get yourself dressed for school. I'll be so happy and proud for you when you do that" and, "Don't be so lazy. You and I both know you can snap your shirt yourself!"

If your child shows signs of having a particular talent or interest, encourage it (see "Let Them Obsess" p. 215). Don't take as gospel the estimated age ranges toy manufacturers list on their packaging. Although you certainly want to heed the small-parts warnings that make some toys unsafe for children under three, there's no reason some three-year-olds can't play with a toy for five-year-olds. It never would have occurred to Michelle to teach her five-year-old son, Chris, to play chess—she knew too much about a five-year-old's limitations. But his grandfather, who neither knew of nor could care less about terms like "age appropriate" noticed one rainy Sunday that Chris was very interested in his chess set. So he sat him down and taught him how to play. Chris loved the game so much that Michelle enrolled him in a chess class.

When Madeline was four her mother, Jocelyn, noticed she could easily and cogently describe the plots of TV shows and videotapes she watched. So Jocelyn expanded her reading material beyond simple picture books. She borrowed *Charlie and the Chocolate Factory* from the library, and sure enough, Madeline sat transfixed for page after page, even though the book was recommended for older children who could read it themselves. Three-year-old Kenny's parents were surprised that he could already bat a ball, ice skate, and do cartwheels while most of his friends were still mastering the concept of "catch."

Not all children who are encouraged to excel will end up out-performing their peers—which is fine, since their performance isn't the point. Allowing your child to feel the pride and pleasure of accomplishment is. Children succeed when their parents support their interests and optimism. We all want our children to blossom, to have as rich and rewarding a life as possible. They will only be able to do this if you infuse them with the spirit and will to do the best they can.

Chapter Three

EIGHT DON'TS FOR THE
INNER PARENT

1. Don't Feel Guilty about Working

If you're a working mother there's a good chance that along with battling exhaustion you're also duking it out with guilt on a daily basis. It's time to stop. Feeling guilty about the time you're away from your kids doesn't just add to your stress and tension, it is also hard on your children. So you have a choice—you can feel guilty about working *and* feel guilty about feeling guilty, or you can get over it.

If you're working because you have to, take comfort in the knowledge that on some level your children understand the sacrifice you are making on their behalf. Perhaps they don't get it now, but they will when they are older. It's a waste of time and precious energy to feel remorse over short-changing your children. Sure you wish you could be with them more, but you're doing the best you can for them—and that's what good parenting is.

If you've chosen to work even though it's not a financial necessity the path to overcoming guilt may be rockier. There's nothing wrong with loving your job and the stimulation, status and/or money it brings you. A major cause of guilt in working parents (or at least working moms) is that although they love their children more than their job, at least some of the time they love being at work more than being at home. But who wouldn't? At "work" you usually get to take a coffee break, have lunch, even go to the bathroom whenever you want. And most bosses don't throw tantrums (or projectile objects) as frequently as your typical tot. Just about anyone would rather spend ten minutes dealing with an irate customer than acting as the one-person clean-up crew when the poopy diaper leaks all over the couch. Add to this the small matter that when you work you get paid, while working as your child's at-home caretaker is a money drain, even if you euphemistically call it an investment in your child's future. No wonder being at the office can feel like down time.

For many working moms the greatest source of guilt is not avoiding all of that stay-at-home scut work, but depriving their children of their presence. Do kids really suffer in the long run if you're gone for eight to ten hours of their earliest days? It seems that for every study that says "yes," another study says "no" or "who knows?". Which means that all you really have to go on is opinion. Mine is that there are real benefits to your children if one parent stays home much of the time until they are school-aged. Young children are wired to look for consistency, to attach themselves to a loving grownup who becomes their beloved, their rock and their center of gravity. If you're that person, your children benefit from your smiley (if sleepy) "Good morning," your strong arms when they turn into twenty-five furious pounds of feet and fists, your warm hug and your firm "No!". They won't get it if they're being raised more by a day-care center or nanny than by you. A kindergarten teacher once told me how heart-wrenching she found it when students in her class would get injured and cry—not for Mommy or Daddy—but for their baby-sitter. "I suppose I should be happy that they have *someone* to cry for," she mused.

Now that I've done my utmost to make you feel really guilty, search your soul. Still want to work? If so, stop torturing yourself. While research is still fuzzy on the pros and cons of growing up in a dual-income family, it should be crystal clear that wallowing in guilt can be detrimental to your child.

For starters, feeling guilty makes it more likely that you'll overindulge your kids and have a harder time being firm when they need it. That's what Maureen, a full-time marketing executive, learned. She let two-year-old Janie sleep with her almost every night because Janie cried dramatically whenever she was tucked into her crib. Maureen understandably worried that Janie was bereft because she wasn't seeing enough of her mom. While it's true that Janie's childhood would have been greatly enriched if her mother were around more often, Maureen's career was not responsible for those nightly waterworks. Many two-year-olds launch major protests at bedtime—even if their moms are always home. But haunted by guilt, Maureen ended up topping off her long, stressful day with a poor night's sleep in the company of a tossing, turning two-year-old. Both of them usually woke up cranky, which made Janie all the more likely to wail when her mom left for work.

Finally, Maureen took a two-week, stay-at-home vacation. Janie was thrilled to spend so much time with her mom, but she still kept up her nightly performance. Why give up when you have a good thing going? Fortunately, Maureen caught on quickly. By the end of the two weeks, she was ready to make Janie's sleeping in her own room a firm bedtime rule.

If you feel guilty about working you're likely to be overly lenient with your kids—and also give them a negative impression of the working world. It's hard to act happy about going to work when your child is clinging desperately to your leg. But sending kids the message that work is onerous to you just compounds the problem. A significant plus for kids who have a working mother is that she can set a great example for them about the joy of work and about the strength of women. Whatever their gender, the children of working mothers may be more likely to view women as at least as capable as men. So if you love what you do, or parts of it or the benefits it brings to you and your family, let your children know. True, kids can gain these pluses if you hold off working (or working full-time) until they are older. But detouring from a career path is not always practical or even possible.

Keep in mind, too, that even if you do stay home, you'll probably need to get away from your kids regularly for your sake and theirs. Though all children probably wish their parents would be available twenty-four hours a day this is neither good for them nor realistic. Very few sane people are constitutionally suited to being full-time (as in twenty-four-hours a day), at-home parents. So if one parent is home much of the time, he or she also needs some kind of sanity-saving outlet, whether it's part-time work, a volunteer job, or field hockey.

The best scenario for *your* child is obviously what works optimally for you. If you do keep working, it will be easier to leave the guilt behind if you send your child the constant message that you love him more than your job. That may sound insultingly obvious, but it's really not. After all, love isn't just something you feel but also something you give. So often, our job gets the best of our attention and devotion while our kids get the leftovers. The short temper, impatience, and apathy bred from exhaustion are more often visited on children than on bosses, customers and clients. This is partially a matter of timing, especially if you work full days. Few people are at their best while they're racing the clock in the morning, or in the evening when they've been doing someone else's bidding all day. So, when you *are* home try to make the most of that time with them. You don't have to devise ambitious quality time projects like trips to the science museum. You just have to focus on your kids rather than your mail.

2. Don't Trust Your Instincts

Mothers are not miraculously born the same day that babies are. Yet many women believe they are supposed to become overnight experts in getting their baby to eat and sleep, and to judge whether his cry means he's hungry, drowsy, uncomfortable or deathly ill. And just where is this expertise supposed to derive from? "Trust your instincts" say the baby-care primers. But a lot of baby care just doesn't have anything to do with instinct.

Take, for example, the notion that you should be able to recognize the difference between your baby's cries. The venerable baby expert Penelope Leach even offers up a spectrograph chart that shows the difference in pitch between a baby's pain cry, basic sobbing and mild, whiny wail. "Maybe you could not describe all these different cries in words. But you will know them apart when you hear them," she writes. Well, my natural mothering instinct failed me completely here. Was it my heart or my ears that were tone deaf? I wondered. Each time my first baby cried it sounded the same to me. I never knew what was wrong, so I comforted him by trial and error. If holding him didn't work, I offered a breast. If he wasn't hungry I tried to burp him, or check his diaper, even take his temperature, or, finally, hand him to his father.

I did finally figure out the differences between my son's cries—but no thanks to me. It was thanks to my son who, at about five months, began to issue distinctive cries depending on the problem. It didn't take any natural instinct to tell that when he screeched he was in pain and when he whimpered he was bored. But until then I suffered miserably, believing that there was something "missing" in me because the language of cries didn't come naturally.

I now know that mommy magic doesn't get sprinkled on you the first time your baby lies curled up in your arms. Motherhood is natural, but that doesn't make it simple. Just ask any new mother who has had to cope with mastitis and engorged breasts and a baby who doesn't seem to know how to latch on. This natural food-delivery system has so many design flaws it has spawned a whole industry of leagues and lactation consultants to help new mothers. Eventually most women (and babies) do learn how to nurse. But the way you learn is by trial and error and by tapping into the knowledge of more experienced hands— whether your mother, in-law, friend, neighbor, etc. You don't learn just by staring deeply at your baby and going with how you feel.

Here's another reason not to mother wholly by instinct. Even if you buy the notion that parenthood is very much a trust-your-gut sort of enterprise, it doesn't necessarily follow that your particular instincts are trustworthy. We all know people whose instincts routinely fail them. There are women who always end up with the wrong man, the wrong haircut, or the wrong job. Their stocks tank as soon as they buy them. We've all had days when we would have benefited from listening closely to our instinct and then proceeding to do the exact opposite.

Instinct may tell you that your child is fine even though she's spiking a 107 fever. She's better off if you call the doctor. Instinct may tell you that he'll be too scared if you let him ride the carousel. But if all of the other kids are going and he's crying because you won't let him, forget your instincts and let him go.

Mothers are often counseled to trust their intuitions because parenthood does go more smoothly if you have a modicum of self-confidence and a belief in yourself. But knowledge figures into the equation, too, and that only comes with time and experience. What almost always does come naturally to new mothers and fathers is a profound, protective, everlasting love for the child. But it can take time and education for that natural force to be channeled the right way. Meanwhile feel free to call *your* mother at six A.M.

3. Don't Be Embarrassed

At two, Jason pronounced the "tr" sound as "f." He also had a fondness for trucks. So you can imagine what his mother's life was like. She'd stroll him around the city and every time he'd see a truck he'd yell that he saw a big you-know-what over and over again, spreading his arms out to show how very big it was. She could have told him to hush up, or tried to correct his pronunciation, or at least gotten him to put his hands down. But that would have just confused him and left him with the vague feeling that Mommy was displeased with him for some reason that he didn't understand. So she just did a lot of grinning and a lot of very loud enunciating, more for the benefit of passersby than her son: "Yes Jason, that is a big T-R-UCK!"

If you embarrass easily, parenthood can be excruciating. The only advice I can give is not to make matters worse by letting your off-spring see your reaction. A young child doesn't know from embarrassment, but is still likely to keep doing whatever is mortifying you just to hear your nervous giggle again—and again. So instead of trying to hush her up, try distraction or a quick, simple explanation. Say you're on the checkout line at the supermarket and your two-year-old daughter says, "Let me see your nipples, Mommy," or asks if you or various other members of the family have penises. The best strategy may be a quick, quiet explanation followed by a distraction (for once you get to be grateful for the candy displays). Sometimes, there's no way out but to politely decline to lift up your shirt or unzip your pants and then explain the word "private" in full earshot of strangers. This may be greeted with great magnanimity by your offspring, or may result in her wailing about your private parts at the top of her lungs. What can you do? Grin (or don't grin) but bear it. She's not intentionally trying to embarrass you. She's just too young to realize that some things are not for public discussion and that, usually, conversations about private body parts fall into that category.

At the top of the list of life's most embarrassing moments with little kids are those triggered by their guileless indiscretion when it comes to another person's unflattering physical flaws. A four-year-old may innocently ask Aunt Joan, "Why are you so fat?" or be fascinated by the tufts of hair growing out of Uncle Joe's ears. Walking down the street he may point at a dwarf, laugh and say loudly, "Mommy, that man looks like a baby!" At a funeral, a three-year-old may walk up to the new widow and ask pointed questions about why her husband died and whether and when she's going to get a new one. One little girl I know announced to her daddy that she was going to marry him when she grew up. "What about marrying me?" her grandfather joked. She gave him a withering look and said, "No. You'll be dead."

Most adults make allowances for the utterings of children—they may chuckle and make reference to "out of the mouth of babes," and all that. But some people really get offended. You can always apologize to them, but it doesn't make sense to scold your child since the hurt was not intentional. Instead, explain to him or her why that man looks like a "baby," and emphasize that it's not a good idea to talk in public about things you think are strange or ugly or funny about other people because that could hurt their feelings. But don't expect to make much headway. Hurting somebody's feelings is too abstract a concept for most children in this age range to grasp. In the meantime, just be grateful for your daughter's innocence and take solace in the knowledge that a decade or so from now, when adolescence hits, your mere existence will be excruciatingly embarrassing to her.

4. Don't Hate Your Baby-sitter

Let's call her Denise. She's warm-hearted and smart with a great sense of humor and oodles of energy. She comes highly qualified with ten checkable references, a driver's license that's cleaner than yours, a certificate in infant CPR and in her spare time (when she's not volunteering at her church) she's working on her masters degree in early childhood education.

If she sounds like the perfect baby-sitter, she is. Which is why if you're lucky enough to find her (and rich enough to pay her what she deserves) and you're the typical imperfect mother, you could come to hate her. The root of that hatred of course is anxiety and jealousy over the fact that she seems better at your job than you are. There she is taking care of your child while you're off taking care of customers who act like children, but that's not quite the same thing. Worse, Denise treats the job as if it isn't "just a job." She seems to genuinely love your kids and most horrible of all they seem to love her back. Your baby coos and kicks his legs when she enters the room, your toddler uses the potty for her but not for you, your five-year-old consumes vast quantities of broccoli in her presence.

Sure you want the best childcare possible for your child, but you don't want to feel like a third wheel. It's hard to give your child's care over to a stranger without wondering whether your child will become more attached to her than you.

Baby-sitters (and great day-care workers, or a mother-in-law with the magic touch when it comes to colic) often become the lightning rod for a new mother's ambivalence about going back to work. Wherever you finally come down on the work, no work or some work decision, here's why you shouldn't hate your baby-sitter:

Your kids love you more than her.

Virtually all little kids love their parents best, assuming their home life is loving (and sadly, when it's not they usually still love their parents). If today he says he loves Denise and he hates you don't believe it. He's probably just trying to push your buttons or express anger because you didn't buy him bubble gum or because he misses you so much.

All kids behave worst around their parents.

Kids are savvy enough to realize that there's a crucial, unalterable difference between Mom and Dad and the world's greatest nanny or day-care center: You are stuck with them while the Denises are not. If they throw their food in Denise's presence there's always the possibility that she could walk. They know you won't. So consider the contrast in their behavior a great sign that they feel safe with you, know your love is unconditional and that no baby-sitter could ever really replace you.

She just seems to be better at the job than you.

If you only had to deal with your children for six, eight or even ten hours a day it would be a lot easier. But parenthood doesn't come in eight-hour shifts. No matter how her day with your child has turned out, when it's over Denise gets to do something you never get to do: She gets to *stop working* while you're only halfway through your workday. Parenthood is always work. It's a lot easier to be patient with little ones when you know there's a time limit. When you're a parent the hours, days, years can stretch out before you like one big, exhausting all-nighter. So it's a lot harder for you than for Denise to think of great projects your kids can make with paper towel rods, sequins and cornstarch or to remember to say *"Please* stop" when your three-year-old daughter is about to turn off your computer.

She knows what not to tell you.

If she's as smart as she seems to be, she hasn't told you that your baby said "Da" for Denise before he ever said "Da" for his Dad. She didn't tell you that he took his official first step while she was in the room and you were on the phone downstairs. The following week, when you announced proudly that Junior said "Da" to his Daddy and that on Sunday you held out your arms and he took his first steps, she simply said, "How wonderful!"

She deserves better.

If you're blessed enough to be able to have somebody so wonderful watching your children you should do your utmost to make her life as happy as possible. Since there's nothing more precious to you than your children your baby-sitter deserves better than being nickeled and dimed or having to deal with your snits over the fact that she forgot you wanted them to have chicken for lunch and gave them pasta instead. Of course, you shouldn't let anything go when it comes to Denise. But don't allow your jealousy to get in the way of dealing with her fairly and professionally.

You can fire her.

The decision is yours. But if you're foolish enough to let her go you and your children will be utterly miserable. And then the person you'll really hate is yourself.

5. Don't Take It Personally

Even if your child isn't the highly talkative type it's unlikely that you'll get through her early childhood without hearing "I hate you" at least once. The first time your child uses the H word in your direction can be shocking. If your child *is* the verbal sort you can expect to hear elaborations on this theme along the lines of: "I hate you, you're a bad guy. I'm going to put you in a box and send you to Chicago. AND DON'T COME BACK!"

How's that for having your soul singed? Kids can say the meanest things once they find out how powerful words are. When your child lashes out you're not likely to think, "Oh good, she's using her words just like I taught her!" Instead, you'll worry that you're raising a little psychopath. But most of all you're likely to feel hurt and rejected. Is this the payback for wiping her bottom, picking the lima beans out of her mixed vegetables, and watching with her for thirty excruciating minutes every morning while the Teletubbies butcher the English language? What did you do to deserve such wrath anyway?

You became a parent. Like it or not there is a difference in the quality, if not the intensity, of the love parents and *young* children feel for each other. Usually, the parent's love is laced with generosity, sacrifice and selflessness. Despite the exhaustion and frustration that come with being a parent, there's sheer joy at the child's mere existence. This helps get you through the bad days and makes the good ones that much better.

But a child's love for a parent comes woven with dependency and self-interest—your child *needs* you. Inevitably, as they grow out of infancy they begin to grapple with these feelings. Psychologists call this learning to separate. It is the process by which a child comes to understand that he is an individual with different thoughts, feelings, ideas and needs than Mommy or Daddy. For many people, separating from the love and authority figures of childhood is a lifelong process. But it certainly begins early. The more a child's mental and physical growth allows for distance from Mom and Dad the more exhilarating and scary life becomes. Part of her wants to cling, part of her wants to fly solo. A lot of the crankiness and nastiness some young children (and teens) direct at their parents is fall-out from this inner struggle. Sometimes she says "I hate you" because voicing that emotion helps give her the inner resolve to separate from you a little more. Sometimes she says it out of anxiety, since it's easier to go to preschool and leave behind your mommy (or get left behind by her when she's off to her office) if you devalue her first. The H word is sometimes a young child's way of saying "I can too leave you because I don't care for you anyway!"

Admittedly, all of this can be extremely hard to take. When your child begins the slow process of separating from you, you're forced to separate from her, even if you don't want to. Gone for good are the dreamy days of infancy when you were the unquestionable light of your child's life. You felt so protective and so close to this little creature as you second-guessed her every move and perhaps even nourished her with milk produced from your own body. She loved you unconditionally, like no one else ever had. And now the dream is over. Standing before you is an angry, snarly little being who is trying with every ounce of strength to push you away.

In some parents this understandably stirs up feelings of insecurity. They wonder if they're doing something wrong. Why else would their darling suddenly be so full of venom? If you're in the throes of self-doubt because your child has announced quite bluntly that she wants a new mommy or daddy and then, after a dramatic pause, that she wants a *better* one, you won't feel the sting so much if you ask her what a better parent than you would be like. From your perspective, of course, a better parent would be endlessly patient, always in high spirits, chockfull of creative ways to teach everything from musical scales to hieroglyphics. *Her* better parent would allow her to squirt shaving cream all over the rug and would consider pink cupcakes and sugar wafers complementary proteins. No wonder she wants to replace you.

You might as well develop a thick skin because it may be years before your child develops the self-control to keep her negative thoughts to herself. Between now and then you may be bombarded with plenty of unflattering assessments of your parenting skills and expressions of deep chagrin at the continuation of your existence. The absolute best thing you can do when your child is grappling with the need to feel more separate from you is not to make a huge deal out of her verbal aggression. If you respond with, "Oh, no. You love your Mommy." Or "What a horrible, nasty thing to say!" you make her feel guilty about wanting to grow up. Yes, you should correct her and teach her to steer clear of sassiness. You could say something like, "Words can hurt, we don't say mean words in our family." (For more advice, see Rule 4 1/2, "But Don't *Just* Talk About Feelings," p. 22.) But at least as important as training her to talk "nicely" is to help her sort out her inner turmoil.

So help her to first label her feelings ("you sound very angry") and her wish ("you wish you could be boss/go to the restaurant all by yourself, etc.). She'll probably be very grateful for your understanding. This doesn't necessarily mean that she'll give up the verbal pyrotechnics—at least not today. But eventually she'll learn to say "I wish I could do it all by myself" instead of wishing outloud for you to be disposed of with a flush, just like her brother's dead goldfish.

By remaining calm and understanding you reassure her that she still has your love and protection, which she desperately needs. She doesn't really want to hurt or destroy you. Deep down she's frightened by her own words. She'll be relieved to discover she really isn't powerful enough to make her darkest wishes come true.

6. Don't Compete Over Your Kids

When Sammy was six weeks old his mother Lucy noticed he was deliberately swatting at a toy that dangled in his crib. True, the toy had been attached to his crib for the express purpose of getting him to swat at it. But the baby books said he wasn't scheduled to start swatting for another month or so. Lucy announced this miracle to all of the women in her new mothers group. Then, At 4 1/2 months Sammy exhibited another sign of wondrous precocity: He sat up. Another announcement to her mother's group. Fast forward to twenty months. "When I grow up I'm going to be a firefighter," Sammy proclaimed. "What amazing verbal skills!" his mother proclaimed to the group.

Lucy was feeling pretty puffed up about Sammy until the next day when she visited a friend whose son was four months younger than hers. This mother had an easy system for keeping track of her children's milestones and the adorable things they did: She would scribble them on a wall calendar hanging in the kitchen. As Lucy sipped some ice water, she scanned the calendar, only to discover that her friend's son had announced his first career choice (airline pilot) two weeks ago. A quick calculation told her that he had crossed this milestone a whopping 4 1/2 *months* ahead of Sammy. Lucy felt deflated. And then, fortunately, she came to her senses and realized she should never have felt *inflated* because of her son's accomplishments.

For some parents it can be a very thin line between feeling proud of their children and being dependent on their kids' successes to feel good about themselves. If you have a friend who is constantly, annoyingly bragging about her kids so much that you're left wondering whether yours are suffering from serious developmental delays, realize a few things: First, she's probably exaggerating. Hyperbole is probably the world's most underreported epidemic and is no doubt genetic. New parents are hardly immune to it. Second, she may be bragging to compensate for feeling really bad about something in her life—or about her kid. Maybe she's worried that her son is still engaging in parallel play when many of the other boys his age at the day-care center are running around exchanging secret handshakes and pretending to be pirate maties. She's trying to convince herself (and everybody else) that everything is fine, so she starts bragging about what a computer whiz he is—already adding and subtracting computer-generated bunnies like a first grader! Don't get angry with her, feel sorry for her. She's worried about her child, and probably needlessly. Over time she'll calm down.

Unfortunately, though, there is a third reason a mother with a young child may keep careful score: She may just be an incorrigibly competitive kind of person. Since she tends to see the world as divided into winners and losers she's going to work very hard to make sure that her child is perceived as a winner, even at your child's expense. The best course of action you can follow is simply to avoid her as much as possible.

If you yourself get competitive about your kids, for whatever reason, you'll eventually figure out that it doesn't make sense to be this way. If you're lucky you'll find this out now, so you'll be way past it by the time you are facing college applications. Being competitive about kids has a very nasty way of backfiring. Take the case of Moe and Joe, two five-year-olds who had tested into their city's magnet school for the gifted and talented. They were good buddies and lived in the same apartment building. But while they spent their mornings building block castles at kindergarten, their mothers were engaged in an intense competition over whose son was smarter. This went on for years, adding increasing tension to Moe and Joe's life, especially on report card day. Finally, in fourth grade they could take it no longer. They skipped school together, spending their allowance in a video arcade. This got them suspended. They did it again, which got them expelled. Everyone learned a very important lesson. Now Moe and Joe go to the neighborhood school and their moms try to focus on their sons' education rather than their percentiles.

If all of the above is not enough to snap you out of competing over your kids, maybe this will: It's not worth keeping score because you can never win. There will always, *always* be someone who can one-up you. Your child walked at nine months? Your neighbor has a nephew who walked at seven. Your child could read "See the cat" on his fourth birthday? Someone else's could read the *Hollywood Reporter*. Your daughter just got into Harvard Law School? Congratulations, your neighbor's kid is going to Harvard Law and getting an MBA at the same time. Your child may never be President of the United States. Or walk on Mars. Or win an Oscar. *But somebody else's will.* So do yourself a favor and come to terms with it now.

7. Don't Judge Other Parents by Their Kids

At times you will be sorely tempted. There's the child who acts outrageously at a birthday party. He grabs and pushes and won't sit still. When his mom reprimands him he throws a mega-tantrum. Tsk-tsk, you think, beaming at your own child, so daintily licking the chocolate frosting off of her fork. But you can't really make assumptions about how wise and loving another child's parents are based on that child's behavior. Kids get to be who they are—and act the way they act on any given day—via a complex equation that combines their parent's guidance with a host of other variables ranging from what they had for breakfast that morning (not to mention *if*), how long they slept last night, the condition of their gums and, most of all, their fundamental temperament.

Research has documented that there are in-born differences in personality. Some little kids are wild, some restrained, some are shy, some are daring. These differences often come down to brain chemistry, not just how good a job their parents do at teaching them social skills and setting limits. A parent's job is to accept a child's fundamental personality in ways that keep the child safe and help him grow up feeling like he and those around him are worthwhile.

You may see plenty of approaches to parenting that you disagree with. But you might feel very differently if that child were yours. Many parents, for example, are horrified when they see young children in leash-like harnesses. It can seem inhumane to tether a child as if he were a Chihuahua. But say your child was a wanderer who, if you turned your back for a moment, would soon be but a speck on the distant horizon. What would you do if you had to go to the airport? Maybe being harnessed gives *that* child, whose parents you see at the ticket counter with twelve suitcases, more freedom than he could safely be offered any other way. I've never harnessed my own children and I'm not advocating the practice—just for having an open mind when you see parenting approaches that don't suit you.

Yes, some parents are truly awful. Acknowledging that some kids are harder to raise than others is not the same as making excuses for bad parenting. It's everybody's obligation to be on the look-out for children who are being harmed by the people they depend on most. But if a child is having behavioral problems you can't *assume* his parents are to blame. Even when kids are very young we are not wholly in control of how they develop.

Rona and Ronnie both have six-month-olds who wake up in the middle of the night and cannot fall back asleep without being held and rocked. Exhausted and demoralized, Rona and Ronnie both head for the bookstore where they end up with the same book and therefore the same advice for solving their baby's sleep problem: Let the infant cry it out. Rona tries this with Adam. The first night he cries so desperately that Rona can barely stand it. Just as she is about to rush into his room, sobbing and full of remorse for her brutality, Adam stops crying. Miraculously, he falls asleep. The entire ordeal took fifteen minutes. The next night it takes five minutes and the next, Adam is able to fall asleep immediately on his own.

You can probably guess what's going to happen to Ronnie. Her baby, Georgia, screams for forty-five minutes the first and only night she attempts this approach. Perhaps if she had let Georgia wail for forty-six minutes she would have fallen asleep on her own, but Ronnie couldn't bear to try. So she fails where Rona succeeded. This doesn't make her a worse mother. But she may very well hear of Rona's success and question her own adequacy—or her baby's.

Differences among kids start in infancy and continue. Two four-year-olds and their dads are lunching at a local diner. The boys start playing with the restaurant's light switch. Both dads are on the case immediately—and so is the manager. All three of these grownups let the boys know that they must not ever touch the light switch again, or they'll have to go home. Everyone sits down and then one of the boys makes a quick dash to turn off the lights again. His dad hauls him out of the restaurant. Is he a worse father than his friend whose son exhibited more self-control? No. He responded properly to his son's behavior.

If you have more than one child you may be less likely to cast aspersions on other parents. You'll have home-grown examples of how wildly different children can be despite being raised under the same general conditions. It's possible to have a child who makes you look like a worse parent than you actually are. But if you're lucky, you'll also have one who makes you look far better.

8. Don't Let the Future Hold You Hostage

Whether your child ends up as Secretary of State or in a state institution, wearing leggings or leg irons is going to depend most of all on how you raise her. The stakes are high, the pressure is on. For all the talk about genetics and peer group influence, most parents know that the buck really stops with them. So parenting is, almost by definition, a goal-oriented pursuit. Your aim is always to pass down to your child the talents, skills and values that help define your own particular definition of success. We impose our hopes and aspirations on our kids because that's part of our job.

But sometimes you have to stop thinking about tomorrow. It's true that our children are in a constant state of *becoming*, but they are also in a constant state of *being* who they are right now. Suggest dance lessons to a four-year-old girl and she's likely to respond with delight. Suggest dance lessons to her as a method of ensuring good posture in adulthood and you may take the plié right out of her.

Likewise, you just can't base all of your parental decisions on its chances of helping junior get into the college of your, er his, choice. Yes it might be wonderful if little Theresa grows up to have a glorious career in the foreign service. But does that really mean that she should be subjected to French lessons at age four when she'd rather be swinging in the park with her friends?

Health is another area where parents become future-obsessed. It will indeed be a liability for your child if he never learns to look after his personal hygiene, but the weight of his future smile does not rest on whether he brushed his teeth *this morning*. Saturated fats may clog his arteries by age fifty if he doesn't watch what he eats. But should you keep him away from the barbecued franks all the other kids at the birthday party are happily gobbling up? No.

It's fine to encourage kids to make healthy eating choices by educating them, presenting them with mostly healthy foods at home and not wolfing down Twinkies in their presence. If you fill his childhood with rigid dietary restrictions all geared to helping him grow up big and strong and he may indeed grow up to have an admirable cholesterol count. But he'll have been so well-trained in worrying about the future that his daily "present" will be colorless. Of course, it's also possible the opposite will occur: He may rebel and reject any notion of future planning, which means he will probably end up overweight and unfulfilled after all.

Usually by age thirty most of us discover the indisputable benefits of moderation. We just have to apply it to those areas of our lives as parents where we go overboard. So, if you want to start preparing Junior for college entrance exams now, good luck to both of you. Just remember that while every child should be read the story of that prudent little squirrel who stored his nuts before the winter, the real key to a rewarding life falls somewhere between gathering acorns and gathering roses while ye may.

Chapter Four

DISCIPLINE

Never Spank

Raising kids really is the oldest job in the world, so you'd think that by now there'd be at least a modicum of consensus about some of the basics. There isn't. Whether to spank a recalcitrant child—much less an incorrigible one—is the classic case in point. The American Academy of Pediatrics and most mainstream experts in early childhood oppose it. But countless parents—some 65 percent according to one survey—still spank their children just as their parents presumably, spanked them. They swear by the method as the one sure cure-all for stopping unruly or dangerous behavior in a hurry.

Who's right? As in most things kid-related I'd give the benefit of the doubt to the parents. Spanking does work. **But you shouldn't do it**. Sometimes effectiveness is besides the point. Ammonia would probably do a great job of cleaning your kids' teeth, but that doesn't make it the method of choice.

There are plenty of reasons not to spank. But experts are misguided when they try to dissuade tenth-generation spankers from continuing the family tradition by claiming it has a lousy success rate. It wouldn't be so popular if it didn't work. No, it isn't foolproof—after all, parents who spank their kids do have to keep on spanking them. But its success rate is on par with more delicate forms of discipline. Which means if you succeed half the time you're way ahead of the game. There is just no surefire way to get kids to behave.

It's understandable why so many parents find spanking appealing. Though not *more* effective than other methods, it is certainly faster. By the time you calmly explain to your three-year-old that punching the cat is *verboten*, and then carry him to his time-out chair and then set the timer for three minutes—a good five minutes has been devoted to teaching him this lesson. If you simple wallop him on the behind you've got the whole thing over with in a good ten seconds.

So why not do it? Because . . .

It may be harmful.

In a four-year study of children ages one to four, Murray Straus, Ph.D. at the University of New Hampshire found that those who were spanked three or more times a week showed an average two-point decline in their IQ by the study's end, while those who were not spanked showed a three-point increase. Straus theorizes that reasoning with little kids rather than spanking them sparks their cognitive development. Straus has also uncovered disturbing trends among children who were spanked. As time went on, they were more likely to become aggressive and/or withdrawn, and engage in anti-social behavior than children who weren't spanked.

It's a short-term solution.

Spanking your kids for playing tug of war with the glass vase will most likely get them to cease and desist. But the point of disciplining kids isn't just to keep you from sweeping up shards of glass. It's to teach them self-control, so they can learn to behave when you're not there. Spanking doesn't teach that. It is so unpleasant that the child learns not to disobey simply to avoid being hurt, not because he has been helped to internalize the rules of proper behavior. In other words, spanking doesn't teach children not to misbehave, it teaches them not to get caught. Gentler methods, on the other hand, help children to internalize the rules so they follow them even when you're not watching. These methods do take longer, but the time will pass more quickly if you remind yourself that the extra minutes are an investment in your children's (and your) future happiness.

It teaches the wrong lesson.

If you spank Johnny for punching his brother you haven't taught him that hurting someone is a bad thing to do. You've taught him that it's okay as long as you're bigger and stronger than your victim, because then you can get away with it. You've reinforced the very behavior you're trying to eradicate.

Some parents who don't spank make an exception when it comes to teaching a safety lesson. A quick thud on the rear certainly adds *oomph* when imparting the message that you never, ever cross the street by yourself or stick your fingers in the fan. But even in these circumstances it's best to stick to non-violent methods.

Maybe in Beaver Cleaver's day a stern pat was harmless. But nowadays young lives are saturated with violent images from computer and video games, TV shows and the evening news. There's a reason why the country's largest toy-store chain has ceased selling toy guns and why parents groups pressured network television into providing violence ratings. There is a growing awareness that kids who are overexposed to violence are more likely to become violent. It's the responsibility of every parent to create a home environment where violence is not tolerated. You can't readily do that if you spank your kid.

It's a slippery slope.

There are many people in the world who have *never*, deep down in the most secret recesses of their exhausted soul had a fleeting fantasy about throwing an impossible child out the window. None of those people are parents. The rest of us harbor the occasional, disturbing fleeting thought about the children who are otherwise at the center of our life and love. That's not because we're bad; it's because we're human. But, being human, almost all of us also have enough self-control and an overwhelming love and instinct to protect our children which, in combo, renders those brief feelings utterly harmless.

But if the world is caving in on you for one reason or another, and you have a habit of spanking your kid, there's always the chance that your hand will get out of hand. Most parents say they don't spank when they're angry.

Maybe they haven't—yet. A child misbehaves. This misbehavior results in grape juice being splattered all over your good suit. Who wouldn't get angry? So how do you draw the line between spanking and physical abuse? The best advice is not to have to worry about the line at all.

It makes them fear you, not revere you.

One of the main goals when you discipline little kids is to set the controls for coping with their teen years. Now is the time to lay that firm foundation that will up the odds that if something's bothering them at age fifteen they'll take your advice (albeit grudgingly) rather than Beavis and Butthead's. So what you want most is for them to understand that they can come to you even when they think they've screwed up. If they fear you, they won't. If they respect you, they may.

Recently I saw a four-year-old girl run down a supermarket aisle even though her father called for her to wait. I watched as she ran—her natural exuberance having gotten the best of her good sense. Then she suddenly caught herself and stopped. A look of fear clouded her face. Even before her dad caught up she had crouched and covered her head, preparing herself for the whack from his rolled up newspaper which did indeed come down hard on her head as soon as he got there. I found this child's prescience heartbreaking—she knew to expect violence from her father. What are the chances that after years of this kind of discipline she will come to her father with worries about sex, drugs or failing trigonometry? And if you think fear of her father's wrath will guarantee that she won't get into trouble in the first place, you've forgotten what it's like to be a teenager.

Keep At It

Good discipline simply means guiding kids toward internalizing survival skills (like not touching sharp things) and social skills (like not throwing sharp things) that they'll need throughout life. I believe the two best discipline techniques are giving children time-outs—having them sit silently for a pre-ordained period of time (usually for as many minutes as their current age)—and showing them that there are consequences for their misguided actions, such as making them mop up the milk that they spilt deliberately. Which approach—or combination of approaches—you take depends on your own values and the circumstances.

For discipline to be effective, however, you have to apply your preferred method consistently. If you're trying to teach a one-year-old not to touch the lamp, but sometimes you remove his hand when he tries and at others you run for the camera because he looks so much like Bam Bam Rubble with the lamp hoisted over his head, the "warning" message is not going to get through. (If you're having trouble being consistent about something like that, save everyone a lot of grief and just remove the lamp altogether.) Likewise, if sometimes you tell her not to grab the pretzel out of your hand and other times you let her take it, she's going to have a much harder time learning not to grab.

Perhaps nowhere does this rule apply more than to taming tantrums. If you give in sometimes but not others, it's no different than if you always give in. Your child figures it's worth the sea of tears and sore larynx in the hopes that this will be one of the times that screaming his head off works.

The more hard-assed you are about these kinds of rules the more readily your children will internalize good behavior. But life being what it is there will be times when you will want to make an exception. It's probably beneficial for kids to know that their parents are not completely rigid. So feel free to be inconsistent on occasion, as long as you:

1. Don't break a rule until it has been strictly enforced for a while. It's much harder for a child to learn a rule if it's only in effect on occasion.
2. Tell the child you're making an exception and explain why. Make it clear that usually he can't drink juice in bed, but since he's sick you're bending the rule today.
3. Be especially tough-minded next time around, since your child will inevitably test the limits of this concept of "exception."

Try not to make exceptions a regular habit. The more consistent you are the easier it will be for your children to learn what you expect of them— and what they should expect of themselves. At first, being consistent can be a trial since your kids may constantly challenge the rule hoping that this time you'll let them get away with it. But if you are very tough at first you won't have to be so tough later. As your kids internalize your rules they challenge them less and less. At first you may need to deliver a series of mini lectures each time your child puts her bare foot atop the dinner table. Eventually, though, just raising your eyebrow will stop her before she starts.

Remember with Whom You're Dealing

If your current method of disciplining your child isn't working at all or is even backfiring, make sure you're fitting your approach to the child, not the crime. When a young child misbehaves most parents react based on their view of the severity of the problem. If it's a minor infraction—like wiping her hands on her jumper instead of her napkin—a gentle verbal reminder will suffice. For more significant no-nos, time-outs usually prevail. And if the child has done something really serious she is taught that there are consequences to such actions—for example having a privilege temporarily removed. So, if Kelly keeps running out into the street, Mom might make her stay inside for an hour while the other kids are playing outdoors.

The problem is that different children respond differently to the same form of discipline. Jules, your neighbor's three-year-old, cries miserably when he is put in the time-out chair for throwing his toy cement mixer at the TV. His misery reassures his mother that he has gotten the message. Afterwards he wipes his eyes, accepts her hug and then resumes his play, being careful not to throw another toy. Time-outs are well-suited for Jules. *Your* three-year-old, however, thinks getting a time-out is a hoot. He sits on his chair giggling, making silly faces. You tell him if he doesn't keep quiet you'll make the time-out longer. He just smirks and then giggles through his second time-out, too. When it's all over, he aims his toy at the TV yet again. Only when you take it away do his tears appear, along with the glimmerings of contrition. For your son, time-outs don't get the message through—consequences do. Then there's your sister who has done away with time-outs completely for her very sensitive daughter Alice. If she's put in a time-out, Alice sobs uncontrollably. Her heart-wrenching tears are punctuated by agonized cries of "No, Mommy, No!" When it's all over she needs to be held and rocked for twice as long as her time-out lasted. These days your sister handles Alice's infractions with some gentle words of admonishment instead.

You can't take a one-size-fits-all approach to raising kids. What works for one may be ineffective or too traumatic for another. Even the same child may respond quite differently depending on the circumstances. The two major causes of misbehavior in young children are hunger and fatigue. When a child gets wild out of sheer exhaustion you compound the problem if you ask him to pick up the books he just swiped off of the shelf. It's better to send him off for a nap (don't *ask* him if he's tired, he'll most likely deny it) or just hold him so he can calm down. Likewise, if he's hungry the solution to his transgression is to have a snack.

In the best of all possible worlds parents would expertly foretell whenever a young child was about to reach meltdown. But since parents are human and so are their kids, there will be times when you get caught having to cope with outrageous behavior that a snack or nap would have prevented. There will also inevitably be times when you come down hard on your kid only to discover that he has a fever. So don't have some pre-ordained method of discipline. Instead, keep a menu in your mind. Before you select which approach to use, look for evidence that the misdeed was fueled more by your child's lack of fuel than by his desire to test your limits.

Of course, you need to be careful not to allow hunger or fatigue to become excuses for misbehavior. You can't allow two sets of rules to exist— one when he's feeling his best and one when he's not. You don't have to let him get away with having hurled all the "Spot" books onto the rug. But it makes sense to let him have a nap before he must pick them up.

Remember that you can judge the success of discipline not by how your child responds during the episode but afterwards. If your approach is leading your child toward greater obedience it may actually be working. But if instead your child cowers or tests your power all the more, try something else.

Don't Have Too Many Rules

See five-year-old Henry. See him come home from Pre-K and break ten of his mother Joan's rules in one minute.

1. He drops his jacket on the floor. "We hang up our jackets," says Mom.
2. He opens the cookie jar. "No cookies before dinner."
3. He takes off his shoes and socks. "Put your socks back on."
4. He dumps his drawerful of super heroes onto the carpet. "No dumping."
5. He whines, "I'm HUNGRY." "No whining."
6. He looks at the orange slices his mom has peeled for him, and says, "I hate oranges." "In this family we don't say 'hate.' "
7. He begins to eat an orange slice. "Wash your hands bef . . ."
8. "But Mommy . . ." "We don't interrupt!"
9. "Sorry." "Don't talk with your mouth full."
10. He cocks his fingers and goes "Boom." "No guns allowed."

You can't fault Joan for her rules. But does she really have to insist on each of them in rapid fire? And in such dictatorial style? No wonder her son wants to shoot her! All kids need restrictions to keep them safe, relatively germ-free and (eventually) capable of civilized behavior. But you need to prioritize based on your values, your child's age right now and current circumstances. Like Henry, most young children err almost constantly. If you hound them about every niggly goof you'll make them miserable and also fail to improve their behavior. Kids have a harder time following rules if you have too many of them. Joan would be better off knocking many of her rules off the list right now, or at least camouflaging them so they sound like suggestions rather than strict regulations. For example:

1. He drops his jacket on the floor. "Where's the best place to put your jacket?" asks Mom.
2. He can't open the cookie jar because Mom keeps it out of reach until snack time. "Can I have a cookie?" he asks. "Yes, after dinner," says Mom.
3. He takes off his shoes and socks. "Your feet will get awfully dirty without socks on. Do you want me to help you put them back on? Or, you could go get your slippers." If he says no, she doesn't push it.
4. He dumps his drawerful of super heroes onto the carpet. She lets him. She already has a rule that he needs to clean up before dinner, so she'll deal with it then.
5. He whines, "I'm HUNGRY." He's whining because he really is hungry. Mom overlooks his tone of voice. "Come, let's go wash your hands, then you can have some orange slices."
6. He says, "I hate oranges." She says, "Are you feeling cranky?"
7. He says, "Yes. I want a cookie." "You may have one *after* dinner," she reminds him.
8. He sighs as if making a major concession, and sits down to eat his orange. She hands him a wet paper towel for washing his hands.

By editing out some of her minor rules about coat hanging and toy dumping, the new and improved Joan makes sure that the message she cares most about—no cookies before dinner—doesn't get lost in the clutter. And, because Henry isn't made to feel so frustrated he is more likely to eat his orange.

Never Use Put-Downs

When your child grows up her life will basically go one way or the other. Either she will be shipwrecked by lousy lovers, dead-end jobs, and habits that are bad for her health, or she will navigate her way past such horrors. The deciding factor in which way she will blow comes down to two words: self-respect. Where will she get this? From you. Now.

Along with imparting to her all of those rules and regulations about covering your mouth when you cough and sharing your toy trains, you also want to discipline her in a way that helps her internalize the message that she's a nice, capable, smart person who's deserving of good things. All loving parents want their children to grow up feeling good about themselves, which is why instilling self-esteem from the get go has become almost a national obsession. So why are so many young people sorely lacking in this basic element of success? A major reason is that too often in the name of guiding our kids we end up putting them down.

Usually, a parent does this by criticizing a child's character instead of just correcting his behavior. A correction is very specific—it focuses on what a child *did*. A criticism focuses on who he *is*. Saying "Pick up those blocks *now*" is a correction. It is one more small step in the ongoing campaign to teach him to clean up after himself. But "Bad boy! Why can't you ever do anything right? I said to pick up those blocks *now*" is a criticism. It might send the message that it's time to put away his toys, but the larger message, of course, is that he's no-good.

Here are some other examples of correcting vs. criticizing:

Correcting: Tommy, say thank you to Grandma.
Criticism: What's the matter with you? Say thank you to Grandma.

Correction: Please stop whining.
Criticism: You spoiled girl! I am sick and tired of listening to you whine.

It's virtually impossible to grow up feeling like a competent, worthwhile person if you constantly receive the message that you're no good. At its extreme, verbal aggression toward a child is a form of abuse that can leave scars as deep as physical abuse. Even if it doesn't go this far, criticizing a child can leave a negative mark on his psyche. What makes this especially sad is that it's easy to avoid this damage if you learn to watch what you say to your child, especially when you're exhausted, frustrated or worried.

If you've gotten into the habit of stepping over the line the first step back is to acknowledge that your child is *never* to blame for your outbursts. Little Leo stared open-mouthed as his mommy bellowed at him to wash his hands. "Why can't you just do what I say? I hate it when you make me yell and say mean things to you."

"But Mommy," said Leo. "I didn't make you yell—you did it all by your-self." Leo's right. It's always *your fault* if you lose it with your child. It's understandable that you get frustrated. But the parent/child relationship is not an equal partnership—we have most of the power, so we get most of the responsibility. In that way it's obviously different from other intimate bonds, like marriage. When criticism becomes rampant between a husband and wife it's often because one of them (usually the one with the TV remote) is being, uh, shall we say, "unresponsive." On their honeymoon the wife says sweetly, "Next time you clip your beard, could you please clean the little hairs out of the sink basin?" But by the first anniversary of her husband's apparent deafness on the subject of beard hairs she has begun screaming, "You disgusting slob, get your damn hairs out of the sink!" The solution is for *both* of them to change. She should stop calling him names and he should start cleaning the sink.

But with a young child the solution to ending criticism is not teamwork. It's simply for you to stop yourself. It will help if you remember that your children aren't closing their ears, acting up, or making you run late because they are out to get you, stupid, or just bound to fail in life. They are doing this because they are children.

The best way to discipline them, therefore, is to correct them straight-forwardly. Eradicate from your arsenal any phrases that step over the line toward character assassination. When your child does something wrong:

Be specific, not global.

Words like "you always," and "you never" are toxic to young ears because they suggest the child has an ongoing character flaw rather than a deficiency that can be fixed. This can become a self-fulfilling prophesy.

So say, "Please try to remember to wipe your face with your napkin," instead of "You are always such a slob."

Correct his behavior, not his character.

Most of all, avoid name-calling as in, "You're such a little cheater, no wonder Charlie doesn't want to play with you." Try, instead: "When you play a game you have to follow the same rules as everybody else." When he throws his truck at the window you say, "You know we don't throw toys at the window. It could break. Now I have to take the truck away for the rest of the day." You don't say, "What's wrong with you, you brat! You'll never see this truck again!"

Stay in the present.

Often, loving parents get critical of their children out of fear for the child's future. As in: "No one will want to be your friend if you're a slob," "How will you ever be able to take care of yourself if you can't remember to brush your teeth?" It can be tempting to vent your worries this way, but these tirades inevitably backfire. What can doom a child to a lifetime of ineptitude is not his current inability to keep up on his oral hygiene but a childhood full of hearing that he can't do anything right.

Don't Ask "Who?"

If you have two or more children it will be nearly impossible to determine which of them is guilty of every minor transgression you uncover. Most of the time it doesn't really matter who left the refrigerator open or the bathroom faucet running or a telltale fingerprint in the cake frosting. Next time the culprit is likely to be the *other* one. Part of being a young child is to stumble from near miss to misadventure day in, day out. Inevitably you screw up. Deliberately or not you break a rule. When you do you should count yourself fortunate if your parent doesn't ask "Who?" but "How?" As in "How did this happen?" and "How can we fix it?"

"Who" singles somebody out for public blame. The result is humiliation, which teaches children very quickly to buck or duck when the "W" word is sent their way. Guilty or innocent, 99.9 percent of the time they will answer, "Not me." Often they will then focus on accusing their sibling or the dog. This is understandable since by asking "who" you let them know your major goal is to point your finger rather than get the problem fixed. This is a fine approach if you want your children to grow up to be the kind of adults who blame others, cover their you know whats at the first whiff of trouble and generally try to avoid being responsible for their actions.

If, on the other hand, you want them to grow up to be problem solvers who don't shrink from responsibility, don't ask "who." Call them both over and point out the problem as in, "The faucet wasn't turned off." If they begin to accuse each other let them know you're not interested in who did it this time but in explaining why it's a problem and discussing what to do about it. "When the faucet gets left on water is wasted. In this house we don't waste water. What should we do now?" Most likely you'll have two volunteers to turn off the faucet. Praise them both, end of story. If one of them keeps forgetting to follow the rule you can brainstorm ways to help him or her remember. Mostly, though, reminding him will be up to you, since life's little daily rituals and routines are not yet second nature to kids this age. If your general approach is to ask "how?" eventually you will get to the point where you can simply call out, "The playroom light was left on" and often the guilty party will say "oops!" and correct the problem.

Most of the time this is the best way to deal with the minor infractions of very young perpetrators. But exceptions abound. There are times when you really do need to know who did something, especially if you know or suspect it was done in defiance (in which case you probably don't really need to ask "Who?" do you?). Sometimes kids need to get called on the carpet for their crimes. But before you holler "Who?" ask yourself: Is this deserving of punishment? If you think the guilty party needs a time-out or other discipline then you need to ask "who." If the goof doesn't measure up to that standard then there's no need to play detective.

Catch Them Being Good

Like most people, little kids are suckers for flattery. This human trait may be a frailty in some circumstances, but it gives parents a great discipline tool. By praising kids when they do the right thing you can short circuit their impulse to do the wrong thing. A well timed, "I like how nicely you're waiting your turn," can abort an impending shoving match. Praising a child for being kind, unselfish, non-violent, patient or just plain quiet when the occasion calls for it is a reward worth doling out generously.

The sad truth is that children often don't get as much praise as they've earned. Bad behavior stands out far more to us because it's just so, well, *noticeable*. Although it's human nature to focus on what's wrong with the picture and glide over what's right, this is a tendency we ought to break for our children's sake. When the day is going smoothly and you feel an impulse to thank heaven for your good fortune, try thanking your child instead. And on rough days keep your radar up for even the smallest praiseworthy thing she does. Tell her you're pleased that she put her shorts on herself, even if they are on backwards. Applaud him for putting the toy drum down instead of throwing it. This sort of positive discipline does more than help children control their negative impulses. It also lets them feel good about themselves when they deserve to—which means it's good for their soul. Too many children grow up with the sinking feeling that they can never do anything right—simply because no one ever notices when they do.

Avoid Giving Negative Attention

Getting noticed for doing something wrong is better than not getting noticed at all. That's a major tenet of childhood and the impetus for a wide spectrum of outrageous behavior.

You can suspect that negative attention is at the root of your own child's incorrigibility today if he or she has a paradoxical reaction to being disciplined fairly—in other words, if it doesn't work. If he leaves his time-out chair only to scatter the pieces of another puzzle all over the floor during clean-up time, it may be he's decided it is better to annoy you than risk your ignoring him.

Sometimes kids who are trying to get a parent's attention will run through their entire repertoire of Most Annoying Behaviors. They will deliberately spill their milk, say they hate you, refuse to brush their teeth and then trip their little brother.

Goaded into action, your first inclination will be to give this child plenty of what he's asking for, depending on the discipline approach you think best. The problem, obviously, is that you don't want him to grow up thinking the way to be noticed is to be a jerk. The solution is simple—you ignore the bad behavior as much as possible and look for some reason, any reason, to give him some positive attention. For example you say, "I'd really love to do that puzzle with you. Why don't you go pick up the pieces and then we can get started?"

If you're just too busy (for example, nursing a new baby) to give him the spotlight right now, let him know that's the case. Acknowledge how tough that can be, how much he must wish he always had your attention. And then make a plan and a promise for some alone time with him very soon—say, after dinner.

If one of your kids is an overachiever when it comes to striving for negative attention, make doubly sure to stick to rule # 3 (p.16) and keep a 5:1 ratio in favor of the positive. Go overboard in tipping the balance in favor of hugs, kisses and good humor and there's a good chance he'll give up his naughty act in a hurry.

Get Over It

"Put that down!" Erica yells. But you're too late. Already her five-year-old, Leonard, has pulled the trigger on his older cousin's rubber-ball launcher which, for all its high-tech bells and whistles follows the same laws of physics as the crossbows of Sherwood Forest: Pull back, aim, push the button and watch the ball shoot across the room. Her nephew uses it for target practice against his bedroom door. But her five-year-old's notion of a bull's eye is *her* eye.

She ends up spending Thanksgiving at the emergency room. Worse than the soreness and the eye bandage she gets to wear for a week is Leonard's attitude toward the whole catastrophe. He has been told many times never to point anything at someone's eye. Yet he seems, shall we say, "casual" about the whole affair. Right now his only misgiving appears to be missing Grandma's pumpkin pie.

Erica is hurt and shocked, but Leonard's attitude is perfectly normal. The concepts of empathy, guilt and right and wrong are just beginning to dawn in children this age—which means you may see only the dimmest glimmerings of them. Leonard is still too young to fully understand his transgression. There's a reason why projectile toys are not meant for five-year-olds. Sympathy and safety sense probably develop in tandem.

So what should Erica do? The easy part is dealing with her son. She should sit down and explain clearly—even angrily—that what he did was wrong. She should devise a fitting punishment (seeing her bandaged may be enough). And then, she should *let it go*. She would do this even if her natural tendency would be to harp on the subject until she elicits from her offspring a degree of remorse that befits his offense. She may not get it—or not in a form that she recognizes. Instead of crying and saying he's sorry, Leonard might hide or be extra silly or clingy or even nonchalant. If she keeps hounding him about it he won't just get the message that what he did was wrong, but that she thinks he is bad. This sets him up to have a negative view of himself that will only bring him—and her—sorrow. Glib as it sounds, she has to make sure he knows that she hates what he did but she still loves him.

Like I said, that's the easy part. The hard part for Erica will be dealing with her own anger, sorrow or guilt. It can be unnerving when your child does you real-world harm. Yours may never land you in the ER—but you are unlikely to get through his childhood without him ever breaking a window, scribbling with a marker on your best pants, or making you so late to work that you get reported. As part of learning right from wrong kids will inevitably do wrong. Consider it part of the learning process: They learn the consequences of their actions and you learn a crucial parenting rule—you have to get over it.

Everyone has a dark side. If you want to see the spectrum of humanity played out in all its intensity—from selfless generosity to callous cruelty— just spend a few minutes at a nursery school. Part of our job as parents, obviously, is to nurture the positive and help our children control and minimize their destructive impulses. It's easier to do this if you don't flip out when the occasional shaft of light illuminates your child's nasty side with horrifying brilliance. That glint in her eye is an ingredient in your child's makeup, but it's not the entire enchilada.

If you're really concerned that your young one is headed for a life of crime headlines, take the following test. Does your preschooler *consistently*:

- Have great difficulty getting along with other children, including engaging in frequent physical fights.

- Intentionally hurt animals.
- Stay riled up even after you've tried to calm him for a few minutes.

Obviously, if the above profile of a troubled child seems to fit yours you should seek help. Otherwise, put your child's error behind him—and you. Kids rise to our expectations. So say something like, "You made a mistake and learned your lesson. I know you'll never do anything like that again. You're a really great kid." What matters aren't the exact words, but the message. The most effective way to keep him from the worst is to let him know over and over again that you expect the best.

Be Deaf to Whining

I know a woman of great patience, good humor and titanium nerves, who can listen to her child whine all day with nary a wince. But most children do not have such a parent and therefore are far better off if they are taught to quit whining. The reason is simple: Whining makes most parents so irritated, frustrated and impatient that they end up whining back. As in:

"Maaaaaaaa."

"Whaaaaat?!"

Volleying whines back and forth with your child is more than a waste of time. It undermines your authority, since you've come down to her level, and it makes it harder for you to be clear, loving and, when necessary, firm.

The only thing to do is to convince your child to stop whining. The best way to do that is to stop hearing it. Let your child know that you don't like whining and therefore will no longer acknowledge any request made at a higher pitch than his standard speaking voice. A simple, "I will no longer be able to hear you when you whine," will suffice. The next time your child whines remind her of the new reality by saying, "I can't hear you." The *next* time she whines use the Socratic method, as in "Why can't I hear you?" The *next* time say outloud to yourself, "Ahh, it's so nice not to be able to hear any whining." As long as you continue to refuse to respond to her until she addresses you in a normal tone of voice you are almost certain to break her addiction to using her voice like a siren.

This method will not end all whining in your home. But total eradication shouldn't be your goal anyway. Everyone is entitled to feel tired and cranky on occasion. Your real aim is to limit the occurrence of those nasal outbursts to the times when your child is feeling genuinely distressed or needy. A child who has been trained not to whine will still let loose when he's upset, but raising the pitch of his voice won't become habit forming.

Give Them Fair Warning

Little children love surprises—as long as they come in the form of a day at the street fair, a cherry lollipop or Mom getting home from work early. But try to spring on them anything that is not delicious or delightful and they are likely to balk. No one gets through childhood without learning that sometimes it's too late to go to the fair, the lollipops are all gone, or Mom has to work late. It can be character-building to face disappointment and learn to cope with it. But just as disappointment is a part of life, so is consideration. And little kids deserve it as much as their elders.

Consideration means not springing bad news on your kids without preparing them. So give a five-minute warning before it's time to leave the playground. Remind her *before* you enter the supermarket that you've come to buy Gouda, eggs and dinner rolls, *not* chocolate bars and Little Mermaid lollipops. You needn't give her a long-winded explanation of the nutritional food pyramid. You just have to remind her of what is not on your shopping list so she's prepared before entering.

Obviously, it's not necessary to follow this rule with a young infant. The typical newborn's attention span is equivalent to the lifecycle of a soap bubble. Even a one-year-old is very distractible, and will quickly forget how much fun he was having running under the sprinklers if you dazzle him with a squeaky rubber turtle and lower him into his car seat or stroller (facing *away* from the sprinklers, of course). But by age two or three, all of this will change thanks to your child's increasingly dexterous memory. Coping with transitions from one activity to another becomes a major challenge. The same kid who at age fifteen will be surfing the web as fast as his fingers can click, may, as a young child, experience systems overload if you schedule finger-painting, making Play-doh, and duck-duck-goose in too-quick succession. And, of course, if this abrupt transition is from good news to bad news—from having a turn playing with your favorite miniature car to letting your buddy have his turn—the challenge may be insurmountable.

How much warning is fair to give depends on the child. But five minutes is a good place to start. Some children do better with ten minutes and some need each passing minute called out to them like a countdown. Just remember that the goal is not to ambush your child with bad news. By preparing her you'll be more likely to leave the playground without your child entertaining the crowd with a demo of pee-wee kickboxing. For her, the long-term payoff will be increased self-control. By offering kids the chance to practice and prepare for unwelcome change, you help them internalize this ability.

As self-evident as this rule may be, you'd be amazed at how easy it is to break. When, on a typical day you're worried about your credit card debt and your father's surgery, your brother's divorce, not to mention your older son's orthodontia appointment which was scheduled for ten minutes ago, you're likely to forget such niceties as a fair warning before leaving the sandbox. You may end up paying for your forgetfulness with a fistful of sand raining down your eyelashes.

It's especially easy to forget to give a young child fair warning when that child is not your firstborn. Since your six-year-old is relatively tolerant of sudden change, you can forget how very difficult switching gears is going to be for his little brother. In such a case, consider the sand-in-your-eye your child's way of reminding you that he really can't act any age other than his own.

For all the benefits of forewarning little kids, there is one trap to avoid. Don't start warning your child about every single disappointment that may occur. Most children are optimists. They will do their best in life if they can hold on to that positive attitude. If you constantly feed them negative thoughts in an effort to cushion them against any downers they may encounter, you will end up teaching them to think negatively. Yes, it's a great idea to let your son know before you buy him that cookie that he can't eat it until after lunch. But if he says, "I just know Daddy will be home for dinner tonight," even though your husband's schedule is uncertain, the best response is "I hope you're right, that would be wonderful," not "Well, you know, Daddy has a big meeting today so he may *not* be home for dinner." Said on occasion, these warnings are harmless. But if you are relentless in your reality-bracing, you can rob your child of his tendency to expect the best—which means he won't have it when he needs it most . . . when he has a three-year-old of his own.

Give Yourself a Time-out

There will be moments when your kids, out of innocence, ignorance, carelessness or deliberate mischievousness, are going to push your detonator button. If you're stressed and exhausted it may not take much to set you off. You have a massive deadline at work and were up past two toiling away. Your spouse is out of town so now it's your job to rush them off to day camp before catching the commuter bus. Probably because they know that something is up they've become the definition of the word balky. Your three-year-old will not use the potty. Your four-year-old will not get dressed because he wants to wear his Spiderman underpants, which are dirty. There is a general revolt against the peanut butter and jelly sandwiches you have just put into their lunch bags. You cajole, plead, issue commands, nothing works. Meanwhile time is passing. Now you have ten minutes to get them both dressed, fed and out the door. They are lying naked on the sofa watching Teletubbies.

The best thing to do in this situation is to remember that time-outs are not just for kids. Tell your children that you're leaving the room for a few minutes. Explain that you're upset and need to calm down. Sit on your bed. Close the bathroom door. Stay away until your pulse rate has returned to normal. For children a time-out is corrective—they get one when they do something wrong. But for a parent a time-out is preventive—it's a calming way to avoid doing wrong by your kids. It defuses a tense situation and gives you a chance to rehearse a more positive approach toward your children's impossible, er, challenging, behavior.

One of the best—and most obvious—reasons for staging this sort of walk-out when you're too upset to think straight is that it will keep you from having regrets. If instead you turn verbally abusive toward your kids, or hit them, you leave a mark on everybody's psyche, including your own. There are few emotions more devastating and impossible to eradicate than parental guilt. And since most parents feel guilty about even minor lapses in their parenting, like not getting their children into the habit of flossing, imagine how it feels once you get to work and look back on the morning's "quality time." Whatever stress was built into your day has just been increased.

Taking a time-out doesn't just avoid a lot of unpleasant self-flagellation later, it also benefits your kids enormously. Removing yourself from the room is a far more effective way to teach your kids self-control than just telling them to calm down. Kids learn more from watching what we do than by listening to what we say. By exiling yourself instead of going ballistic on them you teach them a mature, reasonable way to cope when they're over-whelmed by their feelings. What you're showing them is that just because you feel like throwing something, or saying something mean or pounding your fists into the floor, you don't have to do that. As an added bonus, they'll understand that they aren't "bad" for wanting to hurl their hamburger at their sister—Mommy feels that way too sometimes. But Mommy *doesn't do it*. Eventually that will help them learn not to do it, either.

There are times when leaving the room is not a wise strategy. With a young child you have to balance your own need to calm down against your child's fear of abandonment. You can terrify a two-year-old by walking out on her, especially since she really doesn't understand why you're infuriated just because she has so creatively scribbled over your checkbook. If you must leave a very young child alone put her in a playpen where she can't get hurt.

In most cases, though, taking a time-out can only benefit you and your kids. Usually kids play follow the leader when it comes to attitude adjust-ments. If you're tense and naggy, they get whiney. If you're demanding, they're defiant. If you're playful, often they will be, too. By turning your mood around, you can turn the whole morning around.

If none of the above is enough to convince you to take a time-out maybe this will: It helps you get your way. When you return your children are likely to be far more cooperative, especially if you don't pull this very often. Their antennae will be up. They will be trying to process what just happened and why. In other words, you will have them exactly where you want them. Sit them down and calmly explain again why you left. Then issue your instructions—stay still while I brush your hair, on with your sandals, pick up your lunch box. Be pleasant, make a game out of it if that helps. They will be so relieved to have you back to normal that you may even get them to camp on time.

Leave Food Out of It

If you've been offering your child goodies as a bribe or threatening to withhold them as a punishment—STOP. Using food to manipulate children's behavior can have long-lasting consequences not just for their psyches but also for their cholesterol counts.

Our culture's intense preoccupation with food has contributed to an epidemic of severe food disturbances. A growing number of Americans suffer from obesity and eating disorders like anorexia and bulimia are a continuing problem, especially for young women and girls. Even grade schoolers have been known to obsess over calorie counting. Food is not simply sustenance—it's a guilty pleasure, a comfort in times of stress, a reward we offer or deny ourselves.

To some degree it's probably inevitable that we imbue food with symbolic meaning. There will always be a deep connection in the human heart between nurturance and love. We start out as helpless infants whose sole desire, need, and pleasure is to suckle milk. Throughout childhood plenty of other emotional links between our gastric juices and our brain cells are created. As a parent you want to do your best not to intensify this natural connection. You can accomplish this simply by not using food as a means of discipline. Don't punish bad behavior by withholding dinner, or even dessert. Don't encourage good behavior by dangling an ice cream cone.

It is understandably tempting to use food as a motivator because it is so effective. If your child runs out into the street you want to make a long-lasting impression on her. She's been looking forward to having a cupcake after dinner, so you know that denying it will help her remember not to dart out again. But it will do something else, too. It will heighten all the more the notion that sweets are special (otherwise why would you threaten to take them away?). You will also forge a connection in her head between being denied this treat and your displeasure with her. If her childhood is full of such episodes she will come to equate dessert with feeling loved. Not every child who is disciplined in this manner grows up to drown her work or romantic sorrows by binging on raw cookie dough nor to punish herself by starving. But some will. The way to ensure that yours doesn't is to avoid blazing the trail in her mind between "sinful" foods and punishment in the first place.

Despite the general prohibition against using food to discipline kids there are times when it *does* make sense—namely when food itself is the issue. It is absolutely reasonable to withhold dessert one night if all your daughter has deigned to eat from her dinner plate is the ketchup. You should also remove the french fries if they are deliberately being used as missiles despite your repeated requests for a cease fire. Just be sure you don't use food as a disciplinary tool where it doesn't naturally belong. It's not a wise reward for cleaning one's room or for having cooperated at the dentist. It's fine to spring a surprise trip to the ice cream shop on your kids if you like, but the reason should be that sometimes it's great to have a treat, not because they were quiet while you were on the phone.

Don't be shocked if despite your extreme care in keeping food out of it your kids keep trying to stick it back in. Children themselves often make connections between food and their parent's approval (or lack thereof). When you make their favorite dinner there's a special glow as they hug you. If you announce the need for a punishment your five-year-old might pipe up with, "Does that mean I can't have any Halloween candy tonight?" He has scanned his brain for the worst of all possible punishments and that's what he's come up with. What better proof do you need of the incredible power junk food has on his developing psyche? Your job is to leave the Halloween candy out of it as much as possible. The more he sees it as a big deal the better off he'll be if you don't.

When It Comes to Tantrums
Never Give In (and then when
you do, find a good loophole)

Sometimes, the hardest part of dealing with a tantrum isn't that your child
has (usually in public) turned into a very loud little ball of rage. It's that
your child has turned into a very loud little ball of rage because you blew
it. "Carry me," she says as you leave the supermarket. "No, sweetie," you
say, hardly paying attention. "It's not far. You can walk." Suddenly she's on
the floor by the exit, screaming and kicking her legs. Meanwhile, you're
kicking yourself for saying no. It really isn't a long walk to the car, she's
obviously exhausted, why didn't you just say yes? What you'd really like to
do is pick her up, say you're sorry and tote her to the car. But now you
can't, because that would be giving in to a tantrum, which means the next
tantrum will be even worse since she'll expect you to surrender again.

What do you do? Remind yourself for the future never to respond to a
young child's request before counting to at least ten. Program yourself to
automatically respond: "Let me think about it." (Sometimes that buys you
enough time for her to forget what she asked for anyway.) And what should
you do now? You can wait out the tantrum, then let her trudge sniffling to

the car. Or, come up with a way around the tantrum rule. Feign a misunderstanding. Try something like, "Sweetie, I can't carry you and your teddy bear and all my packages, that's why I said no. If you can hold your teddy bear, Mommy can say yes."

Be aware, though, that this approach introduces the concept of a loophole to children at a very young age. The long-term implications of this remain uncertain. But it's likely to dramatically increase the odds that they will grow up to be lawyers.

Defuse Bad Behavior

Oh what power a young child feels when he gets a reaction out of his parent. So many little-kid antics, like bathroom talk and dropping his pudding-laden spoon onto the just-washed kitchen floor, are intended to see how far he can go and how far *you* will go, to feel triumphant if he gets you to screw up your face in that funny way that makes your eyes look so teeny weenie. Taunting, teasing, goading can become the specialty of any child by the age of three or four. How often your child plays this game with you depends on how much you let him know you don't like it. The more upset you get, the more pudding you will be mopping off your floor. This is not perversity on your child's part. From his perspective there are very few things he can do to try to assert power over monolithic you, to announce he is his own person with a will of his own. So if he sees you blink you're in for it.

The knee-jerk solution is often to become very stern, to warn and threaten, to issue commands and admonitions. Sometimes this works. But always reacting this way backfires in the long run. What you end up teaching is that in the realm of domination you're the winner. What you want to teach is that power games aren't worth the bother.

So here are four gentle ways to short-circuit bad behavior and prevent it from escalating into a scene.

Be silly.

Disappointed that you've decided not to make macaroni and cheese for lunch for the fifth day in a row your son calls you Stupidhead. He says it five times fast. Now he's watching your face with gleeful anticipation. He knows there's a family rule against name-calling. What will you say? Try saying, "Oh, yeah? Well you're a Bupidhead!" There's a good chance he will be reduced to thirty pounds of giggles. Few children this age can resist nonsense words. He may very well come back with "Dupidhead," leading you to retort "Wupidhead," etc. until the bad mood has been broken and he simply digs into his turkey sandwich, the longed for macaroni now forgotten.

Be a broken record.

If, however, he is in a particularly foul mood and nonsense words just won't do, look at him calmly and say simply, "In our family we don't call people names." Not quite what he was hoping for. In an effort to raise your volume he tries again, "Stupidhead!" he screams. In response, don't get excited, get repetitive. Say the same thing again. And then again. After he hears your script three or four times he'll probably get the message, plus the message that you're not going to get dramatic. Most likely he'll give up.

Yawn.

But what if instead of giving up he ups the ante by switching from calling you Stupidhead to calling you Poopyhead? The charm of this approach from his perspective is that it allows him to break two rules at once since you also do not allow bathroom talk to be hurled about. Your best response is to get unresponsive. Stop talking to him. Stretch. Look bored. Look around like you're thinking of chores that need doing. Lose interest and he probably will too.

Ignore.

This is a close cousin to yawning, best used in such circumstances as a trip to the supermarket. "I want this!" "I want that!" Your child's view of which food items should end up in your shopping cart probably diverge from your own in dramatic ways. You can, of course, stop each time your child makes a selection and firmly but lovingly explain why a five-pound bag of barbecued potato chips does not qualify as wholesome lunch fare. You could do this, but it will open the door for negotiations, recriminations, pleas, accusations, and that dreaded of all parental experiences—a Tantrum in Public.

Sometimes the best approach is simply to act like you didn't hear. Keep pushing the cart down the aisle. Often, your child will give up and follow you, only to get distracted by the ice cream freezer. He will forget about the chips and start clamoring for cones instead. Keep going, keep ignoring. Pay attention only when he makes a request you are willing to grant. If he won't leave you alone, just say, "We are not buying candy today. We are not buying candy today." (see "Be a broken record".) Eventually you may get to the car with neither taco chips nor tears.

Now and Then Let
Her Get Away with It

Little chocolate smudges dot your three-year-old's lips and the edge of an orange wrapper peeks out from behind the fichus tree in the living room—tell-tale signs that she has sneaked a peanut butter cup right before dinner. As further evidence her un-wiped hand attempts to hide her mouth as she saunters toward the dinner table. Later, you will chortle with your spouse about her ingenuity—since there are indications that she gained access to the Halloween candy, which was far out of reach, by using a kitchen stool and a chopstick. For now, though, shouldn't you scold her?

Probably. But then again . . . let's say it's been one of those rough days, filled with tears, time-outs or the clingies. Or maybe it's been an incredibly great day—finally she went to day care without howling, waited patiently at your doctor's office, and didn't interrupt your fifteen-minute phone call with your client. Perhaps just this once it may be best to overlook the infraction. Everyone needs an occasional break. If you pretend you didn't notice, you don't have to reprimand her. She gets to feel she put something over on you (and you get educated about how she looks when she has—file it), which lets her feel triumphant.

Do this too often and there's a word for it—spoiling. But if you do it on rare occasion it won't harm her. Just make sure you hold the line the next time she sneaks a candy. You want her to believe that when it comes to catching children's mischief, we parents come equipped with a second pair of eyes in the back of our heads. But you also want her to know that sometimes we blink.

Chapter Five

HELPING THEM LEARN

Read It Again

It's hard to read *Goodnight Moon* fifteen times a day and stay sane. After just one run-through of *Pat the Bunny* I need restraints. Yet reading to kids is crucial to their brain development. And if you're doing it right, your child will probably want you to read the same book again and again. That kind of repetition helps them process what they're hearing and seeing—even if it reduces *your* brain to bologna. Parenthood is hard, and this is just one reason why. Since toddlers, especially, are so distractible, it's tempting to try to get out of another read-through with a quick "Oooo look, flying dust!" along with sleight-of-hand cramming of the book under the couch cushion. Don't do it. Instead, try these boredom survival tactics.

Emphasize Different Words Each Time.

In the *great* green room . . . In the great *green* room . . . In the great green *room* . . . *In* the . . .

Change the Words.

"Little Miss Muppet sat on a puppet." The sillier the better. You spare yourself monotony and your child will probably be delighted to point out your errors.

Skip pages.

Okay, it's cheating. But it's better than skipping the entire book. This works especially well with plotless Dr. Seusses like *Hop on Pop* and *One Fish, Two Fish*.

Choose Classics.

Their longevity isn't just evidence of their popularity with children, but their tolerability to parents.

Ban the Bunny.

Or whichever books are on your personal detestable list. Yes, you should read to your child, but you don't have to read *that* book.

Watch TV with Them

For decades critics have groused about the lousy quality of 95 percent of the TV shows we subject ourselves to every day. So why does television fare never improve? For the simple reason that we keep watching it. Considering our incredibly low standards as a viewing audience (*twenty-four years* of *Wheel of Fortune*!!) it comes as a huge surprise that the one thing many otherwise undiscriminating adults will not abide is watching kids' shows with their children. I don't mean the prime time pablum the networks promote as family shows—I mean the educational (and not always so educational) TV that's directed at little kids.

Okay, so Barney is insufferably sweet and the most dramatic moment on Mr. Rogers comes when he decides whether he'll zip on his blue sweater or his cream one. But you're not watching for your own entertainment or edification. It's a whole different experience when you watch with your child. Kids really can learn their alphabet from Big Bird and good manners from Prairie Dawn. But what they need most is time spent with a loving grown-up, engaged in the show, watching it together, reiterating what's on the screen, asking questions like "What do you think Twinky Winky should do?" or "How many eggs are in Baby Bop's basket?" Also be there to explain images they don't understand, since neither Barney nor Arthur can talk back to them.

As they get older you should continue to watch along with them frequently—especially if you allow them to watch commercial television. By doing so you'll have a great opportunity to teach them another valuable skill—namely, *how* to watch TV. Some parents avoid this tedium by banning TV altogether. But most parents have come to accept that TV is a part of modern life so their kids might as well get used to it.

To prevent TV from turning your child into a dunderhead teach her to watch it critically. Point out the commercial messages between shows. Explain that the toys aren't always as great as they seem in the commercial—that the crayon and the pony depicted on the box aren't really included. When the voiceover announces that some box of sparkly, frosted goodies is nutritious cereal fit for a growing child's daily breakfast, you needn't rant to her about the audacity of throwing 200 grams of sugar into a box and then marketing it to innocent children as nutritious fare. Just point out that on commercials the cereal is always shown next to orange juice, a muffin and milk, for good reason—it's those foods that contain most of the nutrients. The cereal is just (literally) dessert.

By and large, commercial TV for kids is at least as horrible as the adult version. No doubt its real mission is to condition our children's brains to tolerate the mind-numbing shows they will watch in adulthood. By following these tips you'll help your child develop critical-thinking skills. Who knows, someday his adult brain may refuse to listen to another hapless chap say, "I'd like to buy a vowel." If we raise a whole generation this way maybe there will finally be something worth watching for the rest of us.

Don't Rush Them

Walk into any class of four-year-olds and you will see an amazing range of development. One child is able to read. One still can't hold his pencil well enough to write his name. There's a kid who knows that the two moons of Mars are shaped like giant Idaho potatoes. And there's a kid who has trouble remembering to raise his hand when he has something to say. What's even more remarkable about this wide range of development is that it is all found in the very same boy.

By the time they have a preschooler most parents have figured out that there's no such thing as "average." All kids develop rapidly in some areas relative to their peers and lag behind in others. Eventually they all catch up more or less. Usually none of this would be a problem if it weren't for parents. There we go again, worrying because our kid still loves to watch Barney while the one down the block is transfixed by *Magic School Bus*. The best strategy in such a situation is not to worry (ha!) or at least not to worry in front of your child. The worst thing you can do is to push her to learn to read or to give up her trike for a two-wheeler-with-trainers. It doesn't matter if the kid down the block is ready—what matters is whether yours really is.

Partly out of anxiety, and partly out of our work schedules most of us have been guilty of overscheduling our kids. "Keeping up with the Mikeys" I call it. If Mikey is taking karate, shouldn't your son? If he's spending Saturday mornings learning Spanish, *Vamonos*! If he's playing soccer on Sundays, won't your kid be left behind if he isn't there too? If Mikey does fine on drop-off playdates, isn't it just too embarrassing to have to tag along with your son?

It's human nature to want your child to shine. But rushing him sends the message that he isn't measuring up to your standards. You want him to learn for his sake, not yours. This warning goes double for parents who have more than one child. Sometimes a younger one doesn't develop on the same schedule as an older brother or sister. If you had a precocious little girl, you might think her younger brother is surprisingly dull-witted if he doesn't quite have the alphabet down and kindergarten is only four months away. It can be easy to forget all his great traits as you focus on this "lag" (which is only a lag relative to big sister; plenty of very bright kids enter kindergarten not knowing a "p" from a "d").

One woman told me that because her daughter was an early reader, she was concerned that her five-year-old son didn't seem to recognize any words yet. So, she switched from reading him story books and fairy tales at bedtime, to first-grade primers filled with scintillating tales about the cat that sat and the man who said "I can." She read them to him slowly, underlining the words with her fingernail and enunciating them carefully. After a week of this torture her son announced he'd just as soon trade in storytime for a quick kiss goodnight. His mother got the message, went back to reading him fairy tales and *waited*. He learned to read in elementary school just like everybody else and became as accomplished a student as his big sister.

One factor that can make it very difficult to keep calm and patient when your preschooler seems to be lagging is that "real" school is looming. Obviously there's no agreed-upon age at which all children are ready for kindergarten, which is why various school districts and independent schools don't have the same birthday cut off. In some places your child must be five by December 31st of the school year in question. In others the magic date might be August first. If your child has a late birthday but you think he or she is still ready for kindergarten, you might not have a choice but to hold him or her back, depending on the local school rules. But what about the far more common scenario—your child (and usually it's boys who are in question) was born in December. He's on the short side compared with the other kids, doesn't have the same attention span, tends to be a bit clingy. Should you hold him back? Give him another year to grow up?

I don't know what's best for your child. But I do know which factors you should base your decision on and which you should ignore. Observe your child. If he's in preschool speak to his current teachers, talk to the kindergarten teachers. If all signs suggest he's not ready, don't push him just because another Sagittarius who lives down the street is going. Ignore your own sense of let-down, competitiveness, embarrassment. Waiting a year before starting school won't harm your child. Pushing him before he's ready might.

Include Them in Your Chit-Chat

Your idea of a juicy dinner-table topic may be global warming. But if one of your mealtime companions is sitting in a high chair or atop a phone book, save your natural inclinations for another time. Mealtime gets pretty dull to a two-year-old if the adults treat him as if he's furniture or a pet who is addressed only if he has some bodily need requiring attention. By keeping the talk at a pitch a young child can understand you send him the message that he matters—he's an important member of the family. This will go a long way toward building his self-esteem—and, by the way, his vocabulary. Rather than tuning out or acting out because he's bored, he'll soak up a lot of love, attention and new words and ideas along with his gravy.

As tots turn into preschoolers it's even easier to focus meal-time chats on them and their concerns, because their worlds expand. They have friends, interests and an endless store of curiosity. Since they are used to being part of the conversation, this may very well be the occasion for them to ask you some of those priceless questions like how people got invented. Even more importantly, in the rush-rush of their busy days they'll know there's a peaceful, restful time when they can talk to you about what's on their minds. This is a habit that you'll be grateful for down the road when their worries become far more reality-based than whether they can fall down the bathtub drain or the toilet.

But Don't Talk Down to Them

When children are very young we simplify the world of words for them. We call Plaza Street "the street with Alex's house," the office building "the building with the big clock," El Ristorante del Gauchos the restaurant with the tortilla chips. But there comes a time—and for most kids it's by age three—when it's best to call the tape machine the VCR or even the video cassette recorder. Most of them can work it like a pro, so they might as well know its name. Teaching children the real names of places and things is a step forward in demystifying the world for them. It will help him feel grounded if he at least has the proper vocabulary to discuss the places he's been and the things he's seen and done.

Kids benefit enormously if you expose them to grown-up vocabulary. In effect, you become their talking dictionary. You say, "The plane is descending—that means it's going down because we're going to land soon." You say "It's time to go to the departure gate—that's the waiting room near where our plane is parked." Now is also the time to de-cutesify—mostly by getting out some extra "ies" you've put in (as in blankie, doggie, slippies, and toesies). Don't chastise or correct him if he's still calling his bicuspids toothies, but don't refer to them that way yourself.

By age three it's probably also best to talk to him in your normal tone of voice, rather than one high-pitched or sugared-over for his benefit. Though you shouldn't have similar expectations of him as you would an adult conversationalist, you'll help him develop confidence in himself if he observes you speaking to him with the same tone of voice you reserve for the grown-up world. He's not a baby anymore—so there's no need to talk to him as if he is.

Support Their Dreams

When a preschooler maps her career path, the laws of physics, much less the cost of tuition in the twenty-first century, are not relevant factors and shouldn't be. "What a wonderful idea!" you say when she informs you that her goal in life is to be crowned queen of England *and* fairyland. Children are supposed to consider the world a place of infinite possibilities and themselves capable of fulfilling all of their dreams. So when your little careerist wants to talk shop, your job is to encourage him or her: "What will you do when you're queen?" you ask. "You're going to be very busy," you can remark when your child announces she wants to be the president and a waitress.

When children make pronouncements about their future work, part of what they are expressing is their grandiosity. Little kids consider themselves to be the center of the universe. They fervently long to be extremely powerful and capable of doing whatever they want. So, being kids, they do what comes naturally—they turn their wishes into hardcore facts. Even if your son can't run so fast now, he's certain that when he grows up he will be able to run faster than everybody else on earth—even his daddy.

What a child this age doesn't need is for a grownup to try to temper his dreams in order to prepare him for the harsh realities of life. It can be heart wrenching to listen as your four-year-old, whose gross motor skills are not his strong suit, announces his intention to play pro baseball, football and basketball when he grows up. But does it really serve him if you suggest he channel his energies toward accounting instead? Eventually children learn that many things are possible in life—but not everything. Eventually they learn that life may come down to making hard choices, and that sometimes you don't get a choice. But a lot of what happens to us in life depends on our attitude about ourselves. If you want your child to approach life with gusto and rise to the challenges he or she will face, encourage this fantasizing about the future. Tell them they can grow up to be and do anything they want.

Let Them Obsess

Some children go through many "career" changes in the course of a day. At preschool they go happily from sandbox to easel, from story time to dress-up time. But others just can't seem to get enough of one theme, whether it's Martians or dinosaurs, Pooh Bear or road construction. They are really still too young to be hobbyists, but they are nonetheless passionate about their interest.

For his fourth birthday a friend gave Charlie a plastic toy space station and the rest is intergalactic history. Soon Charlie wanted to know all about rocket ships and outer space. He quickly learned the names of the planets. He gave up on his previous career goals (fire fighter, pizza deliverer) in favor of a life spent in intergalactic travel. At preschool he drew space ships, at home he worked on his space ship puzzle, his favorite bedtime book was no longer about wild Max but Anakin Skywalker.

His parents worried some about their little space cadet. From their perspective he seemed a tad young to be specializing. Wouldn't he be better off if his interests were a bit more well-rounded? But his teacher said to leave him alone. Passions are not just normal in young children, they're also beneficial in part because they are such great learning tools.

For one thing, focusing on a passion can help hone a child's memory. She

gets inspired enough to remember that diplodicus is a meat eater but tricer-
atops is not. And though only a handful of youthful dino enthusiasts will end
up digging for dinosaur bones as adults, the mental exercise will help even
if their future is not in paleontology.

Passions can be used to expand a child's horizon. One mother had a
daughter who somehow became hyperfocused on the U.S. presidents. She
could recite many of their names. Her parents used this peculiar passion (for
a four-year-old) to help her develop a variety of skills. They made Play Doh
busts of George Washington, drew pictures of Lincoln and his beard, counted
the number of presidents, talked about the letter sounds their names began
with, etc. If you can take that approach with Grover Cleveland, think what
you can do with trains or fairies!

Your role isn't to enforce an interest in any particular topic but to be
your child's sponsor if one develops naturally. Take your truck lover to
construction sites, your animal lover to the zoo, your budding astronomer
to the planetarium. (Actually, *all* kids benefit from such excursions.) Find
children's books on the beloved topic. Perhaps the greatest benefit of all
these activities isn't the mental stimulation but the love and pride your child
will feel emanating from you. When you take your child's passion seriously
your child understands that you're taking *her* seriously, and that's worth even
more than the great joy she feels when she wears her tutu to ballet class.

If your child's passion suggests an academic proclivity it doesn't mean
you're raising a little Einstein. No matter how smart the child, the passion
is not intellectual in the adult sense. A four-year-old who's fascinated by
knights and castles is interested in the possibilities they offer for fantasy play.
Teaching him about the English royal houses, including the names of all the
Plantagenets, would be wasting your time—and his.

A passion only becomes problematic if the parent's ego gets caught up in
it. There are not only stage mothers out there, but math mothers and football
fathers. Of course you'll be proud if your four-year-old is a puzzle pro or
ice-skating whiz. But if you become too invested in the passion—reminding
your child to practice, inviting all of your friends and relatives to her dance
recital when she'd rather you didn't—it may cease to feel like her thing
anymore, but yours. Instead of the passion leading her to open the doors to

learning she may shut them, out of resentment or growing disinterest. So support the passion, but don't get overly invested in it (who knows how long it will last anyway) or take it as a definitive sign of his future talents or aptitude. For him, the passion isn't about his future career but about weaving his dreams. Letting him feel a sense of ownership over his dreams increases the odds that his future reality will be a bright one.

Skip the Reward

Your three-year-old genius finishes the puzzle in five minutes flat. "Hooray!" you say, enveloping him in a warm hug and rewarding him with a sticker. "I'm so proud of you!" What could be wrong with this? Plenty—if your goal is to encourage your child's development. Just as it is misguided to offer your child false praise it's also a mistake to reward all of his accomplishments.

Although rewards (whether in the form of a lollipop, a sticker or an extra big hug) sound so positive, they have a nasty habit of backfiring. Why? Because they can detract from the love of learning. Children enjoy getting a reward so much that they may begin to focus more on it than on what they were doing. If you consistently reward a child for her accomplishments, she starts to care more about getting the reward than on what she did to earn it. The focus of her excitement shifts from the sheer, natural joy of learning and growing, to pleasing you. If you applaud everytime your child identifies a letter, she may become a praise junkie who eventually becomes less interested in learning the alphabet for its own sake than for hearing you applaud.

Rewards do have a place in early childhood, but don't overdo it. Try to reserve them for motivating kids to better or more grown-up behavior (such as giving a sticker for each morning he dresses himself) or to motivate them to do basic, boring tasks that you don't have to really enjoy to excel at— like brushing your teeth or putting away your toys.

Be especially wary of promising your child a reward ahead of time (whether a kiss or a cracker) for doing something important for her development, like building with blocks. Even very little children come to know that rewards are usually given to encourage you to do something that's onerous or difficult. Promise to reward little kids for their accomplishments and you can inadvertently thwart their inner drive to grow. You turn completing the puzzle (or learning the alphabet or how to swim) into a chore—something they do with one eye on the prize. The classic example of this is paying older kids to read books. You end up instilling a love of money rather than a love of literature.

No, you shouldn't remain poker-faced when your child finally builds her first, four-block tower. But instead of giving her a gold star or going on and on about how proud you are of her, talk animatedly about what she has actually done. Ask her how it feels to have built such a big tower. Help her count the blocks. Ask her what she likes about her monument. Laugh along when she delightedly topples it. Teach her to clap for herself rather than always turning to hear applause from you.

Focus on Friendship, not Penmanship

The first formal decision many parents make about their child's education is whether to send her to preschool, and if so to which one. Recently there has been a push to mandate preschool for four-year-olds, especially those from disadvantaged families. There are many reasons for this, but one of them is to help prepare children for the new, turbo-charged kindergarten. In many ways kindergarten is what first grade was a generation ago. Many children are expected to learn to read, write, add and subtract before they are six. Not all kindergartens have sharpened their academic focus to this degree—some are still just about learning to wait your turn, share crayons, finger-paint and dance the hokey pokey. But in a growing number of school districts kindergartners now come home with homework.

Parents wanting to prepare their children for kindergarten may have a number of options to choose from. But deciding can be confusing because preschools call themselves many different things. Some are labeled "pre-K" programs, others day-care centers and others nursery school. To make matters more confusing, some facilities that call themselves preschools aren't— they are really day-care centers where half the "student" population is still in infancy.

In the days when most families had a stay-at-home parent and a station wagon in the garage, preschool was usually called nursery school. It was attended by children who were three or four and was in session for only a few hours a few days a week. These days you can't differentiate between a preschool and a day-care center by its hours of operation. But you can still identify a preschool by what children do while they are there.

In my book, what qualifies a facility as a preschool is that it offers an educational program. If the facility offers nothing but simple custodial care—the children eat, nap and play under watchful eyes—it's not necessarily a preschool no matter what it calls itself. Real preschools have some sort of organization and schedule, with specific times allotted for, say, story time, meeting, music, snack, free play at various centers, outdoor play, etc. Good preschools also offer a curriculum—in other words, they attempt to teach children about, say, the seasons or animals or holidays in some semblance of an organized fashion. The goal is to serve as a bridge between home and the world of school, to gently guide children toward understanding what school is and what is expected of them while they're there. In many ways, then, preschool should be what kindergarten used to be.

A growing number of school districts provide free preschool. Take advantage if yours does. But if there is no public Pre-K in your district, and you can afford to go private, the trick is choosing the right school for your child. You can drive yourself crazy comparing these schools, especially if you're judging them based on their adult/child ratio, playground equipment, schedule and curriculum, not to mention the SAT scores of the last two decades' graduates. But when you're all done, remember one thing: A preschool is not supposed to be a school, it's supposed to be a *pre* (as in preparation) school. And the school it's supposed to prepare your child for is not Princeton, but the local kindergarten.

So how do you best get young children ready for kindergarten? Let's start with what you *don't* do. You don't make preschool a junior version of the "real" thing. You don't sit the children down at desks and have them recite their ABCs. You don't insist they work on computers. You don't hand out worksheets where they trace numbers. If you have a precocious child who enjoys such pursuits you can offer them at home readily enough. But they aren't what preschool should be about.

The best preschools emphasize social development. They gently teach you that it's okay to be away from your mom or dad or whichever grown-up is currently the love of your life. They guide you toward functioning well as part of a group. Preschool is about bonding with a teacher, sharing, taking turns, using words instead of fists to settle arguments. Yes, there should be some teaching, but the goal ought to be to prepare the kids for a future full of learning, rather than push them into real academics (reading, math, etc.) now. Instead of trying to teach them to read by focusing on the alphabet and the sounds letters make, the teachers should teach *pre*-reading skills. They should read to the children often, which helps them learn that stories have beginnings, middles and ends. For math, instead of getting them to identify the "plus" sign, the teachers should provide blocks, shapes and all kinds of objects that kids can count and sort. There should be arts and crafts to develop their hand and finger muscles (and, of course, their creativity) and plenty of playground play to develop the large muscles in their arms and legs.

Unfortunately, more and more parents, perceiving the world as an increasingly competitive place, put pressure on preschools to be more clearly "educational." They worry that if their child's preschool doesn't emphasize academics, their child will be left behind at the tender age of four. It won't happen. There is a place for teaching a child that "S" makes the "Ssssss" sound and that if you add one and one you get two. That place is called kindergarten.

I'm not suggesting that you reject a preschool because there's a computer in the corner or because you spy a teacher helping an eager child sound out words in a book. The key is what the school emphasizes. Ask what their goal is. If they say it's to make a child's first school experience a happy one, to get them excited about going to school and help them master being separated from their parent or caregiver, that's a good sign. If they proudly show you the worksheets completed by all of their four-year-olds, keep looking. It's a wonderful sign if the school tailors its approach to the kids' individual needs to some degree. A child who wants to learn to write or to read should certainly be encouraged. But most young children aren't ready for that—and it can backfire if you push.

If your child *is* precocious, don't assume that a preschool that emphasizes academics is the best fit. You might overlook some great schools out of fear that they will "bore" your child. Jane almost learned this the hard way. A full-time working mother, she enrolled her three-year-old, Amanda, in her church's preschool. Amanda was very happy there, but Jane was upset when she picked her up one day and noticed that Amanda was doing a very simple six-piece wooden puzzle, the kind that has wooden knobs atop each piece to make them easy to handle. At home, Amanda was a puzzle whiz. She could handle forty- to sixty-piece jigsaw puzzles with astonishing aplomb. So Jane worried that the preschool was not stimulating enough for her. She considered pulling her out, but first she talked to the director, who suggested Jane sit in for a day. Jane did and was surprised and confused by what she saw. She watched Amanda be utterly engaged in activities that at home would bore her. Finally, she realized that what was engaging Amanda was not the puzzle, or listening to the teacher read *Brown Bear, Brown Bear*, or keeping the beat to "Twinkle, Twinkle Little Star" with a drum, but doing all of these things at school with other children. Sitting next to her friend Allison made story time special. Drumming with Ava made music time fun. So Jane wisely kept Amanda at the school.

Moral of the story: When it comes to learning, little kids have great radar. They will hone in on experiences that most obviously meet their need to grow and develop and will quickly lose interest in those that don't. So if your child is really excited about the preschool and loves to go, that's a great sign.

If he or she isn't happy at school, the issue is more complicated. Your child may simply not be ready. There is no magic age by which all children are old enough to be away from home, even for a couple of hours. No law decrees that children must go to preschool. If weeks go by and your child is still miserable, take a break and try again in six months or a year.

Another cause of a child's unhappiness at preschool might be that the school is the wrong fit. You can't make a snap judgement about this. But if your child seems more and more disinterested in going to school, or obviously unhappy about attending, *and* the teacher isn't acting like your partner in figuring out what's going on and making it better, consider looking elsewhere. It may be that the school is pressuring your child to grow up too fast. Remember: The best schools offer children a good start, not a jumpstart.

Click on Exit

In the decades ahead our children will be spending a significant portion of their waking moments interacting with a computer. Hoping to give their kids a leg up, some parents are teaching their babies to click before they can even crawl. Right now our culture is so intoxicated by the promise of cyberspace that we tend to exaggerate its benefits and overlook its down sides. In that way the situation is similar to the emergence of television as a cultural force in the 1950s and 60s. At first parents were thrilled by this entertainment miracle—it was certainly a cheap and easy replacement for that unreliable teenage baby-sitter. I and many of my friends were therefore allowed to spend much of our childhoods staring glassy-eyed at the screen. Eventually our parents realized that although this might be a good way to cultivate Brussels sprouts, it wasn't doing much for our young minds. But by then it was too late. Like so many of my generation I was never able to memorize the periodic tables because my synapses were just too cluttered with flotsam like the theme song to *F-Troop* and the necessity of using fluff, fluff, fluff to make a fluffernutter.

But today, we moms and dads are savvier. Having the luxury of learning from our own parents' mistakes, many of us limit how often our children can watch *Rugrats* and may even declare an all-out ban on *Power Rangers*. Yet many of us are eager to give the *computer* carte blanche to invade our children's brains. Educational software for young ones is a booming business. Just five years ago such products were designed only for school-aged children. Now companies are peddling software targeted at infants.

There's nothing wrong with teaching very young children how to click. Get educated about children's software and you can accrue a good library of games that both entertain and edify. The best of these engage kids in problem-solving adventures rather than dishing out rote memorization games gussied up with lots of digital bells and whistles. (Since pre-readers don't surf the web unsupervised I wouldn't worry so much about the computer exposing your child to aspects of life he—and you—are not ready for.)

Because kids seem to have a natural affinity for computers, these machines can be a great learning aid. But the emphasis should be on *aid*. If you're relying on the computer to teach your children their ABCs, much less their multiplication tables, you're as misguided as parents who once thought they could leave the baby-sitting to Soupy Sales.

Little kids should spend, at most, about thirty minutes a day at the computer. Any more than that can backfire in the long run. The first problem with computer overexposure is that it requires kids to sit for too long. There's not even a commercial break—a pause that refreshes—that would allow children to disconnect from the world on the screen. The result is that, left alone with a computer, a young child is likely to strain his or her back, eyes or hand. I'm sure there are ergonomic solutions to some of these problems, but a tot whose wrist gets a boo-boo from too much mouseplay is having his health held hostage to a microprocessor.

The other big problem with the computer is that sitting in front of the screen is a solitary activity. This may not be true initially when you're teaching your child the rudiments. He or she sits enveloped in your lap while your hand guides those pudgy little fingers in the fine art of double-clicking. But this stage will be shockingly short. The youngest generation is learning to read "start" and "exit" even before mastering "cat" and "hat." By the tender age of four, and even three, many kids are ready to fly solo. If you leave them alone with some fascinating software the silence will be broken by nothing except the muted *click click* of the mouse.

Unfortunately, this cheats children out of time they might otherwise spend bonding with a caregiver and socializing with other kids—the activities that offer the biggest developmental gains of early childhood. A computer only teaches kids how to bond with a machine. It's ironic that from the perspective of social interaction computers are worse for little kids than television. One of the few benefits of watching TV is that it can at least be construed as a social event—and not just on Superbowl Sunday. Families can and often do watch together.

So parents needn't be concerned so much with what their child is doing on the computer, but with what he isn't doing *because* he's playing on the computer. If your goal is to have him develop a love of reading, he is better off hearing you read to him than playing "Reader Rabbit." Love of books and learning will occur naturally if it starts out being associated with warm, cuddly alone-time with Mom or Dad. A computer-graphic rabbit doesn't come close. Little kids learn best by doing, not by viewing. It's important for their whole body to be engaged in an activity, not just their optic nerve and index finger. So, he is better off coloring with crayons than with a color-jet printer and better off stacking his Lincoln Logs than building an on-screen castle.

Which activity should you cut out to make room for the computer? The obvious choice is television! Deduct his computer sessions from the time he would otherwise spend in the company of Batman and Robin or even Mr. Rogers. Whatever you do, don't deduct it from time he would otherwise spend with you. Although children can learn plenty from playing on a computer, the most interactive of software can't give him a fraction of the benefits he'll gain from interacting with you.

Chapter Six

SIBLINGS

Be Scrupulously Fair

No matter what, they will keep score. If one scampers onto your lap, the other will soon follow. She will protest if the pediatrician gives him two stickers and she gets one. He will howl if she collects more Halloween candy than he does. Lord help you if you give one a piggyback ride and not the other. It's easy to get fed up with this nonsense. It's irksome to feel constantly monitored for evidence that you are favoring one over the other. But the sooner you accept the inevitability of their rivalry the better off you and your children will be. The only way to escape your children competing against each other is to have only one child.

Although there's nothing you can do to end their rivalry, you can take the edge off of it by trying very hard to be scrupulously fair. This is because at the heart of their rivalry is the desperate fear that they are not loved as much as the other(s). The typical parent considers his or her love to be as fundamental and abundant as the air—there's more than enough for everyone. But little kids aren't very metaphorical. They live in a concrete world, and from their perspective there's only one of you and at least two of them. This is one math problem they figure out even before they are speaking in three-word sentences.

So do your utmost not to let one feel like the habitual loser. If that means counting out the exact same number of jelly beans, do it. Yes, you can point out to them the ridiculousness of it all and emphasize over and over again that your love (if not your patience) is boundless. But don't expect to make much headway. Again and again they will try to force you to choose one over the other(s). They will both claim it is their turn to get the first ice cream cone. Hand out all of the cones together. Or, insist they work it out themselves before *anyone* gets served. If you surprise your daughter with a Barbie, make sure you have something that's equally special for your son.

Of course, there will be times when you can't give to them equally. The older one *should* get more privileges and responsibilities, the younger one more slack. Sometimes there's only one purple lollipop. And sometimes a child has to endure that most dreadful of events—a sibling's birthday. Cries of "that's not fair" from all quarters are inevitable. The best response is to explain your rationale. "When you were three I helped you clean up just the way I'm helping your brother now." "When you're five you'll go to kindergarten just like your sister." "On your birthday you'll get presents, too."

Following this rule will not completely protect your children from envy— nor should it. Kids do need to learn that inequities exist. But they don't need to learn that lesson from you. The outside world will teach it to them thoroughly, eventually declaring one of them better at chemistry or the clarinet, cartwheels or the backstroke. Like the rest of humanity your children will have to confront the gritty reality that not everything in life is fair. But it will make an enormous difference to them that *you* always try to be.

Remember that It's Hardest
on the Firstborn

It's no fun always living in the shadows—wearing hand-me-downs, riding your big brother's beat-up tricycle, finding two wallet-sized pictures of yourself tucked among two hundred and fifty 8x10s documenting every moment of your big sister's toothless period. Each new milestone you reach—from walking to getting your driver's license—is likely to elicit a dull response from the rest of your family. Mommy and Daddy broadcasted your big brother's first steps with a degree of fanfare usually reserved for a papal visit. But now they don't consider *your* initiation into bipedalism worth an e-mail to Grandma.

But kid brothers and sisters of all ages can take comfort in knowing that when it comes to sibling rivalry, they've already won. No matter how slighted and marginalized the secondborn may feel at times it's the older kid who gets the raw end of the deal. The younger child may not enjoy feeling like an afterthought, but that's nothing compared with the deep, heart-wrenching challenge facing a firstborn when he discovers he's no longer alone on the throne. This is true no matter how fair-minded the parents are. It's true even if they somewhat favor the older child. Sibling rivalry is normal and natural—but that doesn't mean it's always harmless. The outcome of anyone's childhood is dependent on a complex cocktail of family dynamics— not just birth order and spacing but the lifestyle, values and the personalities of everyone involved. Still, when you're all done weighing it out—the inevitable, primal issues of sibling rivalry are mostly the big brother's issues.

It makes sense that this would be so. The firstborn is forced to share his parent's love with someone else. No young child is good at sharing—and sharing your parents is far harder than taking turns with a Tonka truck. You can profess your equal love for both children. But from the first-born's vantage point he's on the losing end of all this diapering and rocking and nursing and cooing. The inevitable result is going to be some degree of hostility toward the baby. This can play itself out in a million unique, eccentric ways. It may be especially intense if the parents don't handle the situation wisely and sensitively (and sometimes, even if they do). Whether the older one transforms himself into Mommy's fastidious little helper or is caught overtly attempting to throw the baby into the trash compactor the cause is the same. The hostility is always there—even if it's mixed together with deep feelings of brotherly love.

The problem this creates for the firstborn is far greater than the trouble it makes for the new baby (provided an adult intervenes before she gets really hurt). That's because Mom and Dad will be none too pleased when their older kid punches this helpless little infant. The older child soon gets the message that his hostility is a bad thing, which raises the anxiety that Mommy and Daddy may think that he's bad, which means he's unlovable, which makes him despise the baby all the more since everything was pretty much paradise before she showed up and ruined his life. This is a lot of baggage for a young kid to be hauling around.

Although children of any age can feel a devastating sense of loss at the arrival of a rival, close spacing between kids seems to sharpen the intensity of negative feelings. This is often so even if the baby is born before the older one is capable of much long-term memory. It's true that he may soon forget that he ever had Mom and Dad to himself and therefore won't be as resentful. But he will also be far less able to express any jealousy he does feel. Instead, he's likely to act it out in all of those unpleasant ways that are more likely to get him a time-out than time alone with Mommy or Daddy.

Close spacing also requires the older child to act like a bigger boy before he's ready. A two-year-old is still a baby. But when there's a new baby in the house it's hard to let him keep that role going for as long as he comfortably needs to. His crib, his diaper pail, his chewed up board books are soon bequeathed to this little bald intruder. As proud as he may feel about his new big-boy status, deep down he's going to feel like something has been lost.

If the kids are close in age the older one will someday face another challenge—his younger brother or sister may catch up and even outshine him. Maybe she learns to read before he does, or can swing the baseball bat with superior accuracy. Sure it's hard to feel outshined by an older brother or sister, but it's far more humiliating to be surpassed by a younger one.

No matter what the children's spacing, the first born is likely to suffer more for another reason—his parents are less experienced. All subsequent kids are on the better end of Mom and Dad's learning curve. Often parents are stricter, more controlling and more involved in a firstborn's early development. The home is an empty slate when it comes to rules and approaches to discipline. So, for example, the firstborn may not be allowed to crawl on the kitchen floor because it's dirty. His parents may react quite dramatically the first time he says "I hate you." They may insist on rigidly scheduled naps, meal times and bedtimes. By the time Number Two Son is crawling, there's so much chaos in the house that many rules go by the wayside, to everybody's relief. So at a younger age the secondborn gets to ride a bike, take soccer lessons and watch sit-coms containing sexual innuendoes. This just adds to his big brother's sense that the world is unjust.

All of this will inevitably leave an indelible mark on a little psyche. But the result needn't be disastrous. Many firstborns thrive. They grow up to be responsible, nurturing and brimming with leadership qualities. This is more likely to occur if their parents recognize just how huge a challenge is being foisted on those little shoulders—and keep it in mind whenever big brother knocks over his sister's castle blocks.

The key to helping the older child will be to offer him a safe haven for expressing his feelings—and to make sure he understands he's not being punished for them. For example, at Aunt Judy's wedding reception five-year-old Nathaniel suddenly wallops his three-year-old sister. You ask him why. "Brittany was being bad," he says.

"What did she do?" you ask again.

"She dances better than me," is the simple, heart-wrenching answer. So of course you're going to give him the no-punching lecture and perhaps a time-out. But if that's all you give him it will just make things worse. You also need to talk to him about what he's feeling. Tell him you understand that it's hard when his younger sister seems to do something better than he does. If you had similar experiences when you were young tell him about them. Let him know that dancing is for fun, it doesn't matter who's better. In other words, when the older one acts up, don't act outraged. Remember that he's not being bad, he's just trying to cope with one of the greatest challenges a person ever faces.

Let the Little One Be Little

For better and worse, a young child with a big brother or sister tends to be worldlier than her sand box pals. She is likely to know at an earlier age about the dreaded powers of kryptonite and to insist she's ready for nail polish before she can even pronounce it. She may even know the names of some of the planets and inform you that everything is made out of "mole-cubes." But worldliness is not the same as maturity. Because she acts like such a big girl sometimes her parents may forget that she's only three. They get stern or impatient when she displays behaviors they would have been understanding about in her brother at that age—like dawdling and whining and lying and refusing to share.

Frequently a household with two children ends up centering its activities and expectations at the older one's level. Since Joe's now big enough to watch Saturday morning cartoons, Chloe ends up seeing them, too. She gets exposed to a higher dose of TV violence and commercials than her brother did at her age. And, since big brother is no longer tolerant of Big Bird or King Friday, little sister doesn't get to see as much educational TV as he did. It's not just TV viewing that's different for a younger child, of course. She gets to eat bologna sooner, and stay up later and maybe even go to summer camp before he did. Younger children are often given more freedom.

But they're also at risk for feeling like they don't measure up because Mom and Dad's expectations are too high. It's easy to forget what a three-year-old is like when your older child is seven.

The closer in age your children are, the more difficult it probably is to be patient when your younger one acts her age. Although you felt triumphant with each milestone your firstborn passed, it can feel like drudgery to go through it again—mopping the puddle just outside the bathroom door, mealtimes that end with more food on the linoleum than in her stomach. What makes it extra hard is that your younger child is so close to being, well, older. In tastes and interests a three-year-old is not unlike a kindergartner. But there are crucial differences. Your typical five- or six-year-old has far better impulse control than a child still in nursery school. "Wait for me, don't get into that elevator," you say as you linger at the handbags display at the department store. A six-year-old can usually obey that order. But for a three-year-old a big, shiny elevator with rows of buttons may be too tempting to resist. Whose fault is it when your child is suddenly heading down alone to the bargain basement? Would you have ever let the same thing happen when your firstborn was three?

It's easy to forget just how fleeting an attention span younger children have. Although listening in on big sister's story time can be an enriching experience for your younger daughter, it may also be too much to ask of her. If she can't sit still to hear the Boxcar children's latest adventure don't scold. Instead, switch-off. The little one does a puzzle while you read Dr. Doolittle, then the bigger one fends for herself while you itemize, once again, what caused the Very Hungry Caterpillar's bout of indigestion.

Is all of this twice as much work? Yes, for the obvious reason that you now have twice as many children. This would be a good time to take a look at any journal or memorabilia you collected during your first child's early years—not just to wallow in sweet memories but to remind yourself that at three your firstborn also had tantrums and nightmares and refused to eat any food that was yellow or green. Cut your younger child some slack. Make an effort to gear at least some of the day's activities to her. Leave Cookie Monster on even if the big one groans. Turn off the TV or make a taking-turns schedule. And give the younger one a bedtime based on when *her* body is tired, not big sister's. By that time she's probably giddy with exhaustion which means she's either being wild, tearful or nasty—and so are you.

Often, second children are determined to keep up with the big kids, which can complicate your attempts to stop them from trying to grow up too fast. The best approach is to pay lip service to her desire to be big, but give her a free ride when it comes to your expectations. If she's ready and able to tackle a two-wheeler with training wheels, let her. But if she tries and fails don't rub it in by saying that the bike is for bigger girls. Instead, diplomatically point out a shiny red tricycle and tell her how lucky she is because it is just her size. Let her try to pour her juice herself, but don't scold if it spills. Insist on clean-up time, but don't hold her to the same exacting standards you do big sister. If she mistakenly throws her Duplo blocks into the Legos bucket, praise her for clearing her toys off the floor.

Despite her sophisticated airs you can still gauge her emotional needs by her birthday. Call her Big Girl but still cuddle with her. Talk to her about Barbie but still give her teddy bears. Even if she'd like to forget how little she is, she'll benefit from having parents who remember.

Have Zero Tolerance for Violence

In the beginning it's the youngest who is in danger. Any number of harrowing events may occur. Perhaps big brother decides it's time to feed the baby—pebbles. Or drag her back to the hospital, head first. Or lovingly rearrange her bedding so that the blankie rests atop her nose. Or just not see her bassinet as he careers through your bedroom in pursuit of imaginary pirates.

Yes, you should use words to remind the older one over and over again about the safety rules. But that's not enough. This is not a criticism of your older child—it's just an acknowledgment of his very young age. All parents shudder at the thought of one of their children seriously harming the other—whether out of malice or ignorance. The obvious solution is to stop shuddering about what could happen and do your utmost to make sure that it doesn't. The only protection against true, tragic disaster is constant, complete vigilance. Never leave them in a room alone together. And when you're in that room with them keep your eye on them, not the hockey game.

Soon, the younger one will become just as dangerous to her big brother as he is to her. That helpless gurgling creature who can't even roll over will be charging up your hallway like it's LeMans. Long before she has the capacity to distinguish between good and evil she will sprout built-in weaponry in the form of teeth and nails. And so—more out of ignorance than malice—she will attempt to bite her older sibling, and/or scratch him, and/or wrap a Christmas ribbon around his neck. It's time to shift to phase two of the sibling protection plan, which sounds exactly like phase one: Never leave them in a room alone together.

Eventually you'll get to stage three. They will both be old enough to know better but they will still hurt each other. You can leave them in a room together, of course, but within five minutes expect to hear cries and shouting followed by both of them bounding up the stairs in an effort to be first to give you their version of events.

Since you can't stop your kids from arguing, you might as well not waste your time trying. But you do need to teach them that they must not hurt each other. Institute a zero-tolerance policy toward hitting, punching, kicking, etc. Make sure you respond consistently whenever one deliberately attempts to harm the other. *How* you discipline each offense will depend on the child's age and the circumstances, of course. A verbal reminder that hitting is not allowed may suffice for standard scuffles. But if one throws a rock at the other you want to make a stronger impression by, say, taking away a privilege (and the rock) if she is old enough to understand the concept of consequences. Most of all avoid spanking (see p. 161). A child cannot "get" the message that violence is forbidden if you hit him.

Although it's crucial to discipline kids firmly when they are violent, don't expect your message of peace to get through any time soon. Violence and poor impulse control come pre-packaged with childhood. But responsible parenting doesn't mean you just accept your child's childish nature. You can *understand* that a four-year-old who punches someone else is not guilty of assault and battery like a forty-year-old would be. But it's still your job to guide him away from childish responses so that eventually he'll stop before his fist hits flesh. He will learn this, eventually, if you discipline him this time, and the next time and the next. If you send your children the constant, unbending message that you find such behavior unacceptable, eventually, they will too.

Do Not Allow Freedom of Speech

In due time, some children discover that it is far more effective to hurt each other with words than with muscles. At first, they will combine these two forms of weaponry. Your daughter's mouth will let fly "Stupid!" while her fist lets fly a left jab. But one day, probably between the ages of three and five, her arsenal may become almost wholly verbal. Siblings become masters at well-targeted teasing, going right for each other's vulnerable underbelly. They will call each other fatty, wimp, whatever insult seems to stick.

A major reason some kids switch from kicks to taunts is that words are more socially acceptable. Too often, Dad just rolls his eyes when one calls the other "blimp" or "dumbo." But if they start kicking each other, he intervenes. This is misguided. Words hurt plenty. A sibling who harps cruelly on the other's flaws—real or imaginary—can have a lifelong negative effect on his brother or sister's sense of worth. Deliberately hurting someone's feelings over and over again is really a form of abuse. It should be no more acceptable in your household for one child to hurl verbal missiles at the other than it would be for him to hurl paperweights.

Most preschoolers don't yet have the verbal facility to get very colorful and specific in their taunts. But there's no reason to wait until their ability in this area blossoms. Let them know now that it's not okay to use words to hurt someone's feelings.

Long before they are educated about the Magna Carta, John Locke and inalienable rights, make sure they already know that in your home there is a limit to freedom of speech. They can *think* what they want about each other. But using their ever-increasing vocabularies to harmful effect will lead to discipline just as readily as would a kick in the shins.

At the same time, you have to help the intended victim learn to ignore these verbal grenades. Teach her that feigning never to hear her sister's taunts, even if they've hit a bullseye, will probably help limit the frequency with which they are uttered. It's just not as much fun to insult someone who always turns a deaf ear, no matter how creative you get at your put-downs. However, as a defensive measure ignoring it only goes so far. Teasers sometimes become intoxicated with the sound of their own voice—there's *some* pleasure in verbal aggression even if you don't elicit a reaction from your victim. So saying nasty things about a brother or sister can become a constant refrain. Truth is, often both siblings are victims since they end up hurling insults back and forth as a form of defensive offense.

That's why the parent's role is to protect them from themselves and each other by enforcing strict rules against character assassination. When they get older they may challenge your right to silence them, invoking the bill of rights as their defense. But stick to your guns. Let them know that in your family calling someone "fatty" is the same as yelling "fire" in the proverbial crowded theater.

Don't Insist on Love

Sometimes siblings act like they don't like each other because, in fact, they *don't* like each other. The reason is nothing more complex or basic than differences in their personalities. Thrown together as college roommates or office mates they'd probably display the same mutual antipathy you see every night at your dinner table. This can make parents understandably sad. But worse than the sadness can be the pressure they put on the two little ones to love each other. "Hug your brother." "Tell your sister you love her." This will certainly stir emotions in your children—like guilt and resentment. But it won't conjure up love.

The sibling bond develops or it doesn't. Sometimes it isn't there at the beginning but kicks in later on in life. Sometimes the opposite happens. So many factors play into the dynamics of human relationships that you just never know. But it will help everyone in your household get along better if you don't try to force a feeling on your children.

Encouraging affection, of course, is another story. You do that by not playing favorites, since nothing will make one sibling resent another more than feeling like an also-ran. Express bountiful delight whenever they are affectionate, supportive, generous or loyal toward one another. Speak warmly about your own brothers and sisters. Emphasize through your actions and stories the importance of family.

But don't tell them how to feel. If your subtle prodding doesn't instill love between the two of them, there may be nothing you can do but accept it. Focus more on helping them each grow up to be good, loving people in their own right. To that end, while you can't insist on love, you must insist on civilized behavior. Most parents do this naturally—they try to create an environment in which all of their children grow up feeling adequately loved and nurtured with an abundance of self-esteem. For that reason it is imperative that you intervene when your children hurt each other physically or emotionally. Punches and name-calling really shouldn't be tolerated.

Beyond that you can only hope that over time and with mutual experiences they will come to see value in the connection they have with each other. Most likely they will—but if they don't it doesn't mean that you have failed as a parent or that your children have failed as human beings. It's more important that they grow up feeling loved by you than forced to love each other.

Don't Be the Judge

If your children come to you with tales of each other's infamy, it is not your job to find out who threw the first punch or was holding the Barbie before the grabfest started. It is oh so tempting to sit down and insist that each child calmly—and as clearly as age and agitation level permit—give his or her version of events. Then you could send down the parental ruling: You go first. It's your turn. You get the timeout. But unless you actually witnessed the transgression with your own eyes you can never know for sure who is the guilty party. And frankly, the larger volume of tears is not always the hallmark of the true victim. When siblings fight they are usually both to blame. When they retell their version of events you discover they can parse themselves out of a jam as well as the shrewdest Washington spinmeister.

It's sensible, therefore, to avoid being cast in the role of judge. Instead you try to coach them in the rudiments of conflict resolution. You do this by using the following tactics, in ascending order of intervention—if the first approach doesn't cut it, try the next.

1. Distract them. A huge percentage of sibling squabbles occur because they can't think of anything better to do. Setting up their train

tracks, taking down a puzzle or saying, "Who wants to color Easter eggs?" even if it's October may get them to forget their outrage.

2. Act wholly unimpressed with either of their tales of woe (unless you've actually seen the crime committed or one child is clearly hurt). Don't stifle a yawn. Say, "Uh-huh, well just play nicely now, children" or some other mindless, boring parental phrase. When they see that your blood pressure is staying decidedly low they may just go about their business and work it out for themselves.

3. *Tell* them to work it out for themselves. You do this by saying, "Work it out amongst yourselves." If necessary, wave your arms around as a visual aid.

4. *Help* them to work it out for themselves. Unfortunately, more often than not this is the tactic you will have to take—at least while they are newly verbal. You do this by putting down your magazine and holding up your hands sagely, shaking them slightly to signal that you're not really listening to either of them, you're just waiting for them to be quiet so that they can hear your advice. Then, in judge-like fashion, you get each of them to give their side of the story, one at a time. But instead of giving them a verdict, you throw the problem back at them to solve. For example: "Well, it sounds like Jinny is upset that Leigh took her Bitty Baby without asking. And it sounds like Leigh is upset that Jinny wouldn't play with her. Hmm, what should you do about this?" Their first answers will probably be laced with self-interest. "Leigh should give me back my doll," Jinny will say. "But *I* want a turn," Jinny will sniffle. But eventually with continued coaching from you, including, for example, asking them what their preschool teacher or baby-sitter would tell them to do, they will finally settle on some semblance of a fair arrangement involving sharing and turn-taking.

This method doesn't work all of the time, nor does it apply to every sibling skirmish. But then, nothing does. More often than not, however, when you recuse yourself from judge-and-jury duty you force your children to resolve their differences themselves. Not only does this teach them important life skills that will help them navigate smoothly through future social endeavors, but it also dramatically increases the odds that you will actually get to finish reading your magazine.

Give Them a Common Enemy

When little brothers and sisters fight sometimes the underlying issue really is who gets to play the plastic xylophone or choose a videotape. But very often their squabbles have little to do with the details and everything to do with you. Each squabble is really about vying for your love and attention. Sometimes you can quell sibling spats by making sure your children get equal shares of the aforementioned, along with frequent, cozy talks about the permanency of their place in your heart. Send this message clearly and consistently through your words and actions and they may not pick on each other much.

But they probably still will. Once again it's time to feed the goldfish. There is the usual mad dash for the jar of food, followed by a tug of war punctuated by ever shriller pronouncements that "it's my turn!" Often "Mommy (or Daddy) said so" will be thrown in for good measure, with a pleading glance thrown your way. Each of them hopes, of course, that you will intervene, proclaim him the winner of the food contest (and your love) so he can then triumphantly feed the fish while the defeated one sulks off knowing he will always be second best.

But since you do no such thing, the scene comes to its obvious conclusion entailing fish food raining down on your kitchen floor and two screaming children both simultaneously trying to kill each other and to accuse the other of fratricide. They will then attempt to draw you into a lengthy "who started it?" debate in which each other's most heinous crimes "He call me stupid!" "She pull my hair!" are dramatically itemized in an attempt to sway you.

When your kids are at each other's throat they can't think clearly, so trying to help them work it out for themselves would be a waste of time. Instead, try to trigger their sense of solidarity. The best approach is an age-old one. Give them a common enemy: you. Simply discipline them together. Force them to be a team by putting them in the same boat. Let them know that if *either* of them starts in, they'll ruin it for both of them. (After all, there's usually enough guilt to go around when these scrimmages arise.) "If anyone punches the other, there will be time-outs for everybody!" "I don't care who threw the fish food on the floor, the two of you clean it up before it's too late to go to the park." "If either of you throws anything, *no one* is watching Barney." Be sure you follow through on your warnings. It's amazing the camaraderie that develops once siblings languish together in a time-out.

Keep Your Childhood Out of Theirs

You were born, your brother asked when you were going back. You walked, he pushed you down. It was your birthday, he stole your toys. He schemed endlessly to cheat, humiliate and dominate you. Then, suddenly, at age eighteen you walked into the kitchen and he said, "I'm toasting English muffins. Want one?" You nodded and thought, "His therapy must be working."

These days you and your brother get along fine. But needless to say the childhood scars you suffered at his hands left you with a highly developed sympathy for the downtrodden and oppressed. This has been a boon in your flourishing career as a public interest lawyer. But as a parent it can be something of a liability.

Your three-year-old and five-year-old have just returned from trick-or-treating. You inspect their candy, but then only half listen as they begin their lengthy bargaining and negotiating session. When they're done, however, you note a marked difference in the size of their candy piles in favor, of course, of your older daughter's. Close interrogation reveals why. She has craftily convinced her younger sister that one peanut M&M is a fair trade for an entire Snicker's bar. She has also told her kid sister that she's too little to eat Tootsie Pops, even though you said they were okay. "Do you want to grow up big and strong?" she warns. Little sister nods, wide-eyed with fear. "Then give me that," the older one says, snatching the lollipop away.

If this scene didn't play like a script out of your own childhood it would be very easy to handle. You would simply tell your older child that this is not okay. You would throw in some homilies about fairness and make it clear to your younger child that she didn't have to trade if she didn't want to. Then you'd watch closely as the renegotiations commenced and, finally, you'd offer up praise all around when their piles looked even.

But since you are still smarting from childhood you may be more likely to be outraged. You see history repeating—the cruelty, the trickery, the future therapy bills. Your baggage is bigger than both of their candy bags combined so you come down very hard. You make your older child feel like a bad guy and the little one feel like a victim.

Permutations of this scenario are being played out in households across the globe. It is inevitable that the ups and downs of our own childhoods will haunt us as adults and inevitably influence how we react to our children. This is especially true if your family is similar in number of kids and gender to the one you grew up in. It becomes so easy to presume the same dynamics will prevail. And, to a certain degree they probably will. This is because in almost all families there is some tension between the kids. They squabble. Sometimes (most of the time) they are both out of line. Sometimes one of them has really done something for which he or she needs an extra dose of parental correction. In which case you should certainly dole it out.

But it can be harmful to our children's relationship with each other (and, of course, with us) if we take sides based upon our own sibling history. The damage this can cause is innumerable. Because your big brother was so domineering you're on extra-alert when it comes to your son being bossy with his little sister. But your daughter's personality is not an echo of yours. Where you were introverted and fearful, she is bold and feisty. More often than not she is bossing around her big brother. But since you are looking at their relationship through the lens of your own childhood you don't see that it's your son who needs extra help asserting himself. Instead, you come down hard on him any time he does get up the nerve to kick his kid sister out of his room. Or, say that your little sister was an awful whiner and squealer who went to great lengths to get you into trouble for the most trivial offenses. It doesn't follow that your youngest is a tiresome tattle-tale just because he announces that his big brother called him "stupid."

The key to leaving your childhood out of your children's isn't to forget your own experiences. It is to make wise use of them. You can't do this if you respond emotionally like the child you once were. Draw an imaginary emotional line—put your children on one side of it and yourself on the other. Every time you find traces of your own past in their doings with each other remind yourself that that was then and this is now. Then you were the child, but now you are the parent. Do this and you'll be able to use the insights you've garnered from your own childhood to help your children in a productive, even-handed way. You may even develop enough perspective to develop some sympathy for your older brother. Who knows? Maybe he wouldn't have been such a horrible beast toward you if you hadn't been such an insufferable pest.

Chapter Seven

BOYS AND GIRLS

Accept It: It's Biology, Stupid

Many parents who have at least one child of each gender find it a hoot when supposed experts proclaim that fundamental differences between boys and girls are rooted in upbringing and culture, not chromosomes. Let's end this ridiculous debate once and for all. Cultural biases may effect how children *feel* about being a boy or a girl and so, in a roundabout way, influence their behavior as well. But gender differences are biological pure and simple.

Yes, there are exceptions to "gender norms." But let's give the majority some air time: Your standard little boy is more aggressive and active than your standard little girl. His favorite fantasy play has a lot to do with getting rid of the bad guy—or being one. He tends to be enthralled with cars, trucks and construction sites. By age 2 1/2 he (and therefore you) may become surprisingly well-versed in the lexicon of trucking, able to identify a backhoe at first sight. He appears to have a magnet in his brain that draws him to anything shaped even remotely like a gun.

Your standard-issue girl really does enjoy domestic pursuits more than boys do. All things pink and sparkly may appeal. Her favorite fantasy games tend to revolve around homey themes, like taking care of a baby, or being a bride. She'll enjoy drawing rainbows at least as much as romping around like a Power Ranger. Barbie rules.

Just when this programming kicks in depends on the child. So if you subscribe to the theory that all of this has to do with *social* programming and are patting yourself on the back because your three-year-old son shows no interest in the deployment of weaponry, just wait. One day he'll probably cock his thumb and forefinger at you in that distinctive way. Likewise, your two-year-old girl may now be content to play along with her older brothers, helping their toy knights slay that green plastic dragon. But someday while the big boys are in school she will rename their dragon Puff and henceforth it will go on picnics with her Madeline doll.

Of course there's enormous middle ground between the genders. Boys will play house, girls will play cops and robbers. And among both genders there's a broad spectrum. There are very girlish girls and there are "tomboys." There are boys who love nothing better than running around the backyard like maniacs and others who prefer a proper tea party.

Accepting that many differences between kids are biological doesn't mean that children should be expected to conform to what is standard for their gender. They are supposed to be children, not cookie cutters. All of us have qualities that would be considered traditionally masculine and feminine. Children benefit when they are allowed to express both sides of themselves. In fact, children are helped the most when their parents accept that gender is biological *and* help their kids stretch beyond it in the interest of becoming well-rounded. The end result of such an upbringing is women and men who can both run the dishwasher and for the senate.

In your effort to help your kids see beyond gender you can expect two major obstacles. The first is our culture. From birth, babies are typecast depending on their sex chromosomes. So anxious are we about the ambiguous gender of those hairless newborns that we color-code them. Heaven help you if you dress your baby son in his big sister's hand-me-down pinks. You only need to look at a typical layette to see society's disparate expectations of boys and girls. Baby boy clothes are designed with active motifs like boats or cars or football helmets. Girls get pretty—and passive—flowers and lambs.

The second obstacle is your child. By preschool, many children become notorious sexists. Because gender is such a central aspect of human life, young children spend enormous energy trying to figure out what it means to be a boy or girl. As part of their learning process they tend to exaggerate gender differences. They may come up with very strict rules about what males or females do—even if these assumptions fly in the face of their own experience. A boy whose mother is a pediatrician may still declare that only men can be doctors. At two a little boy might enjoy twirling around in a tutu. By his seventh birthday, his prima ballerina days will be well over.

The parent's role in all of this is to first, provide some gentle reality checks about the wider choices now available to both genders. In the years before feminism became a household word my father already knew what it took to keep girls from limiting their horizons. When I was five he sat me down and asked, "What can a man do that a woman can't?" I offered up a long list that, along with garbage-collecting and fire-fighting, also included writing books. He shook his head and said, "A woman can do anything a man can do except for one thing." When he saw I was stumped he added, "She can't be a father." I still remember how astonished I was to hear that my options were virtually limitless.

The second thing parents should do is to be respectful when their son or daughter engages in play that happens to be traditional for their gender. Let her wear sequins and play house. Let him be Spiderman and build skyscrapers. Offer them opportunities to expand their horizons, but don't force them. Get your son a baby doll, but don't be horrified if it gets used for target practice. Likewise, go ahead and surprise your daughter with a construction set. But if she doesn't develop an interest in it, don't leave her with the feeling she has disappointed you. There's nothing wrong with being girlish if that's what she wants to be. Whether she grows up to be the leader of the free world won't depend on whether she liked to play with boy toys as a child. But it will depend on her brains, moxy, and how good and proud she is to be herself (and of course, her knack for fundraising).

Get Help for a Child Who's Confused

It's one thing to acknowledge that most girls really do have a penchant for patent leather party shoes. It's another to insist that your daughter wear them if she happens to be one who doesn't. Likewise, it's no sin for a son not to want to be a Super Hero or to prefer floral pajamas to Buzz Lightyear ones.

Still, if your child is clearly identifying with the opposite gender instead of his or her own your job isn't just to sit back and say "What will be, will be." First, you have to find out why your child seems to be breaking the pattern. You need to find this out whether you're devastated or think it's just fine that your four-year-old son wants to dress up every day as a princess.

At times, gender confusion is a symptom of something else. For example, if his new baby sister seems to get so much more attention, a young boy may decide Mom and Dad like girls better than boys, and therefore transform himself in an attempt to regain his monopoly on their love. Responding sensitively—and sometimes seeking help from a capable therapist—can help a child sort it all out. In some cases, there's probably a biological reason why a child just doesn't fit with others of his or her sex. In the years ahead, the playground can become a ruthless place for such children. The solution is, again, to find an empathic and capable therapist who can help them navigate the many social landmines ahead. The goal should be to increase the odds they will grow up feeling good about themselves. Of course, it takes more than a therapist to ensure that happens. Most of all, it takes loving parents. If your child fits into this category, getting over your disappointment may be a lifelong challenge. But it's one you need to tackle since your attitude toward your child is likely to determine his attitude toward himself.

Help Your Daughter Find Heroines

It may not be a man's world anymore, but when it comes to the media it is still a boy's. Hollywood has figured out that although girls are willing to watch films and TV shows focused on and featuring boys, young males rarely return the favor. This is why girls and positive stories about them are underrepresented on the big screen and the little one. The desire for the highest audience share has reduced 51 percent of the human population to tokenism.

Critics point out that even when Hollywood does offer up girl characters they are often depicted in a negative way—or at least in a manner that offers a limited view of females and their interests. For example, critics of the Disney cartoon heroines complain they are unusually intent on getting their man. Fairy tales appeal to many little girls, and there's certainly nothing wrong with them fueling their fantasies by watching G-rated love stories.

But if you want to expose your daughter to a wider range of female characters, get her hooked on books while she's young. They are filled with what films are not: lots of great girls. Here's a brief list of readily available picture books for preschoolers that feature girls (they are great to read to boys, too). This roster is just a start and can be readily expanded with the help of a librarian or experienced bookstore clerk. *Lilly's Plastic Purple Purse* by Kevin Henkes, *Amazing Grace* by Mary Hoffman, The Madeline series by

Ludwig Bemelmans, the Angelina series by Katharine Holabird, the Maisy books by Lucy Cousins, the Frances books by Russell Hoban.

Once your daughter is old enough to read independently (and even before that, if you follow the wise strategy of reading to her regularly) she will find more sophisticated stories filled with girls who have feelings and thoughts she can identify with, and those whose accomplishments will send her a fuller picture of her own great capabilities. A sampling of some classic great books for girls are: *The Wizard of Oz* by L. Frank Baum, *Alice in Wonderland* by Lewis Carroll, the Little House series by Laura Ingalls Wilder, *Harriet the Spy* by Louise Fitzhugh, *Anne of Green Gables* by Lucy Laud Montgomery, *Black Beauty* by Anna Sewell, *Little Women* by Louisa May Alcott. Also check out books in the American Girl series by the Pleasant Company and those by Beverly Cleary.

Once she's old enough to read for herself she's also old enough for you to clue her in about why girls are so unpopular with media moguls. Help her avoid succumbing to the notion that the world is mostly by, for and about males. Do all of this and you will produce a savvy daughter whose self-esteem cannot be trampled by the Nielsen ratings.

Teach Her that Words Can Hurt

Yes, of course you should teach boys the same thing. But nasty words aimed to exclude another child ("Go away." "You can't come to my birthday party." "I don't want to play with *you*.") are far more often the province of four-year-old (and up) girls. When little boys turn aggressive they tend to throw punches. Girls prefer verbal explosives.

In a typical preschool the supervising adults will be on the case immediately if children get into a *physical* fight. The brawlers are given the loud and concrete message that hitting and otherwise hurting each other's bodies is not allowed. But too often when girls use their words to hurt each other, adults don't respond as clearly or firmly. Often, verbal slights go by unnoticed—except by the victim.

Thanks to researcher Nicki Crick, Ph.D. at the University of Minnesota at St. Paul's there's now a phrase for these hurtful words that are meant to manipulate or exclude another child: *relational aggression*. In preschool through to high school, frequent interactions of this type are associated with difficulty making friends, depression and anxiety both for the children who like to dish it out and those on the receiving end.

There's no need to panic that your child will be a social misfit just because, at four, she has a tendency to disinvite friends to her birthday party. Relational aggression is as normal in preschool as are fisticuffs. It's all part of the hunger for more power and control over your life. Once young children discover that words can have a dramatic effect on others they may become weapons of choice. The key is what *you* do when your daughter behaves this way.

The tricky part about intervening is knowing when not to. There can be a fine line between relational aggression and a girl simply expressing her anger. It can be harmful to girls (and boys) to get the message that it isn't "nice" to be angry. Anger is a normal and (if properly channeled) healthy human emotion. It does more harm if it gets repressed than if she lets it out. Too often, parents tolerate anger in a boy but not a girl. It is fine, normal and healthy for a young girl to let a friend (or parent) know that she's upset over something. As she gets older you can guide her toward lowering the volume—or even keeping her fuming to herself, depending on the circumstances. For now, though, consider it a major plus if she uses her words rather than her fists to let off steam.

But venting anger is not the same as deliberately saying something to hurt another person. When a child is motivated by malice, it's time to draw the line for her. You don't have to let loose with a lecture—a few choice words will usually do the trick. The best approach is to let her know that saying mean things is neither a nice nor effective way to get what you want and that it could make other children not want to play with you. With this sort of guidance your child is likely to outgrow the tendency to zing her friends or manipulate them verbally.

If your child is the one being bullied in this way, it's also worth taking seriously. Keep an ear cocked so you can intervene during playdates (or any time of the day if the victim and perpetrator are siblings). Teach your child to speak up and let the other child know that she doesn't like being talked to that way. If the episodes are happening outside your own home, speak to the supervising adult and galvanize him or her to take this sort of aggression seriously—for the sake of both children.

Be Tolerant of Your Little Gun-Lover

Even if you have a strict ban on toy guns at home there's a 99.9 percent chance that your three- to six-year-old son will make his own using whatever natural resources are available to him including sticks, bananas, French fries or your hair dryer. Why boys are so drawn to weaponry is both one of life's deepest mysteries and as plain as the nose on your face. They love guns because they are boys. So you might as well give up now trying to stop this behavior. If you punish them for concocting pretend guns you might as well punish them for being boys.

You don't have to allow bonafide toy guns into your house. Considering how truly dangerous real guns are, there's something disturbing about giving a child a mock one to play with—not because this is likely to turn him into a murderer but because it sends the wrong message to him about what values you cherish. You want him to know that in the real world guns are so often used for evil ends that it's just not a good idea to make up games about them.

That said, if you have a child who is desperately, constantly clamoring for a toy gun you're probably better off caving (see "Give In" p.72). His desire will be less likely to blossom into an obsession if he isn't denied what he so craves. In this case try to get a gun that is the least like a real one as possible—for example, a neon-colored water pistol. This is an important safety rule (toy guns can be mistaken for real ones, with tragic consequences) that will also help him distinguish between play fighting and the real thing.

If, like me, you're a mother who grew up in a girls-only household, you may be initially horrified by the typical boy's fascination with violence. Tolerance! Your job isn't to stop him from pretending he's a Megajammer space warrior but to set limits on his rough housing so that pretend fighting doesn't devolve into the real thing. One of the major challenges facing kids of this age is to learn how to express aggression through socially acceptable activities—i.e., in forms they can get away with. Playing it out is the prime approach. It teaches kids how to enjoyably express the thrill of victory and control without really hurting anyone else. It's not the parent's role to encourage such play. But you also shouldn't chastise your child for expressing aggression in this way.

Of course, that's not all you have to do. You also need to teach him your values and guide him accordingly. Don't applaud his wild antics. If he wants to name the puppy "Killer" you don't have to agree. If he likes to play war, you can, on quiet occasions, talk to him about how very sad and scary real wars are.

There are warning signs that your child needs extra help controlling his desire to hurt or overpower others (see p. 182). But in most cases you needn't over-worry about his love of guns. You're not raising a psychopath, but a normal five-year-old boy. It's just that on some days it can be hard to tell the difference.

Let Him Cry

For the past two decades there has been plenty of "discourse" on the subject of gender roles, the importance of sexual equality, and the fairness inherent in adding more stalls to public restrooms for women. One thing all of this talk hasn't done, however, has been to change the plight of boys. Usually, they are still forced to put on a show of strength and bravado no matter how sad or scared they feel. The same parents who respond with text-book empathy and validation when their daughter gets tearful over scratching her knee send a less sympathetic message when her brother is the one with the bruise. He is far more likely to be told not to cry, that it wasn't such a big deal, and to be praised if he can get his upper lip to stop quivering.

It's time to stop raising boys to be ashamed of their soft emotions. The result of this "Big Boys Don't Cry" approach is that too many men lead an emotionally restricted life. Terrified of public humiliation, they walk around wearing emotional body armor—never crying or hugging, afraid even to sniffle at the movies. This is not being strong, this is being strait-jacketed.

The social prohibition against men showing their soft underbelly is so entrenched that it is unlikely you can spare your son from it completely. But by making your home a safe haven for his softer side, you ensure that his armor doesn't get super-glued on. You do this simply by allowing him to express the *entire* spectrum of human emotions without being judgmental. (See "Rule # 4: Talk about Feelings, p.19) You raise him to understand that people can feel more than one emotion at the same time—you can be both scared and courageous, for example.

Many parents think this all sounds fine in theory but worry that really raising their son this way will turn him into a wuss. But extensive research into emotional intelligence suggests that a boy who is raised to feel comfortable expressing the full range of feelings at home does better socially than others. Because he is aware of his own emotions he is more perceptive than the typical kid in sussing out the social dynamics of various situations. If the soccer coach yells at him for missing the goal during practice he may very well cry about it when he recounts the event later for your listening pleasure. But he is not likely to cry in front of the team.

A boy who understands and accepts his own feelings is primed to experience his life fully. So make sure you create a home atmosphere in which your son feels comfortable rather than ashamed if he feels like crying. Sometimes it helps boys open up if you talk while doing something else together that serves as a distraction—like digging rocks in the backyard, pushing the baby's stroller or drawing cars. Your job is to be ready and available to listen to him—not to *force* him to talk about his feelings. Some boys just don't like to—whether due to social programming or simply the way many male brains are hard-wired. If your son squirms away from heart to hearts don't force them on him. Just make sure you help him to label his feelings and send the message that they are okay with you—which means that deep down they'll be okay with him, too.

Teach Respect for Girls

The days of "boys will be boys" are over. Behavior toward girls that a generation ago would have been met with a chuckle is becoming socially unacceptable, not to mention, illegal. The Supreme Court has made it clear that school districts cannot knowingly tolerate severe, student-to-student sexual taunting. It's now understood that girls have the right to be educated in an environment free of put-downs by sexually aggressive boys.

There have certainly been some backlashes in response to this new legal and social emphasis on student sexual harassment. Some media pundits pounce gleefully whenever an overly zealous principal calls in the cops because a young boy tried to kiss a girl or chanted that he'd seen her underpants. Of course it's absurd to arrest a young child for a crime he can't even pronounce much less knowingly commit. But the truth is that there are some new basic rules of etiquette that boys must be taught. They shouldn't be branded as criminals if they chant "boo girls" in the pre-school playground, but they should be stopped. If the adults in their lives take this concern seriously, boys will come to see it as serious as well.

The time to begin teaching boys proper behavior toward girls isn't when they reach kindergarten, it is at home while they are very, very young. It's our responsibility to make sure our sons enter society with a fundamental understanding that females are just as valued as males and that it is not okay to tease or taunt someone because their gender is different from yours, anymore than it would be okay to be nasty about their skin color or religion.

Most young children pay no heed to whether a friend is male or female, just as they pretty much ignore each other's race. Such differences are irrelevant to them unless someone older teaches them otherwise. So the first line of defence against raising a sexually aggressive son is to teach tolerance by practicing it. Don't suggest by your words or actions that boys are in any way better than girls, or that your son should only play with little boys. When he comes home from Jackson's house chanting, "Boys rule, girls drool," talk to him about it just as you would about any other bad habit he's picked up "out there." Let him know that what he's saying is mean and therefore not acceptable. Point out that girls are kids, too, and have the very same feelings he does.

Also teach him to be respectful toward other people's bodies, including girls' bodies. It's perfectly fine for him and Becky to play chase-and-kiss games in the playground if they both want to. But if *either* of them says no, the game must end. If he's tickling his sister and she yells "no more!" remind him that he must listen to what she's saying—he may not touch someone else's body if he's asked not to. Tell him to apologize. If necessary, use concrete consequences—like having to leave the playground or the birthday party—in order to teach these lessons.

Do all of this as a standard, matter-of-fact part of his upbringing. Don't single him out—teach your daughters the same lessons. Most of all, don't act toward him as though he is fundamentally bad or has latent criminal tendencies that you are working extra hard to counter. You don't want him to think badly about himself. You just want to indoctrinate him in the need for tolerance and respect now. That way, when puberty arrives, he'll naturally avoid the kind of sexual behavior that isn't just troubling, but can also get him into serious trouble.

Chapter Eight

FOR COUPLES:
BEING PARENTS TOGETHER

Don't Judge Your Marriage
While Sleep-Deprived

Nothing brings out the fault lines in a relationship like the joy of having a new baby. You're so exhausted, you find yourself shrieking at your beloved for putting the cream cheese on the wrong shelf in the fridge. Meanwhile your mate is having a tantrum because the instructions for the "easy-to-assemble" crib are only in Italian which is, of course, your fault. And so it goes. You read the advice in the baby books not to neglect your marriage and to find time to go out together. So there the two of you are at the Chez Casa Mia Inn, equipped with a beeper and enough quarters to call the baby-sitter between every other bite. One of you is doing just that, and then returns only to find the other's head bobbing gently over the radicchio.

Some 60 percent of couples experience a drop in marital happiness upon the arrival of parenthood. There are understandable reasons for this, most having to do with very real differences of opinion concerning how the baby should be cared for and by whom. Typically, wives complain that their husbands aren't doing enough, while men feel they should be applauded for how much they *are* doing, especially compared with their own fathers whose only childcare role was to be baby's emcee as in, "Honey, he's crying again!"

Husbands feel cheated as their alone-time with their wife gets crowded out by the baby's endless, desperate needs. And then, of course, there are always the endless expenses a baby requires that unnerve you further. To top it all off your entire value structure—what you think is important in life and what you feel "eh" about—shifts dramatically once the Mantle of Parenthood is wrapped around your shoulders.

A lot of the marital tensions a newborn brings to the fore are rooted in serious issues. But they loom extra large when you're exhausted. So if you're giving (or receiving) the silent treatment from your spouse or if you see yourselves transforming into an updated version of The Lockhorns don't despair. What your marriage needs more than anything else right now is sleep. Yes, hire a baby-sitter, but skip the night out. Sleep in instead. Do this often enough and your spouse's flaws, which now seem so severe and entrenched they threaten the core of your marriage, may once again become tolerable, even adorable, foibles. At least until the return of PMS.

Create a Privacy Zone

When you have little kids the boundary between being a couple and being a family can get blurry. This is understandable. Since your children are a part of you and an expression of your love, you put them at center stage. Even if you didn't do this naturally, they'd still find ways to hog the spotlight. There they are again. When they are not the topic of conversation they are interrupting your conversation. They crawl into your bed, impose themselves in the middle of a hug, and generally conduct themselves as if your sole function on earth is to be their parents.

If you have kids you have a loving obligation to put them ahead of your selfish needs and desires, to sacrifice for them and commit to raising them as best you can. But part of being a parent is teaching children about privacy. They have to come to understand that as special as your bond with them is you have a different sort of bond with your mate which takes precedence. To do this you need to enforce boundaries. Just as you don't overly intrude on your child's world, you don't allow your child to intrude on yours. You say, "Please don't interrupt, I'm talking to Daddy now." And, "Mommy and Daddy need some privacy now." Or "Mommy and Daddy are going out, just the two of us because that's something that grown-ups who love each other like to do." You let them see you celebrate your love. You talk glowingly of each other to them. You let them know how special your spouse is to you. Yes, you celebrate Daddy's birthday as a family. But then Mom and Dad also do something separate.

Many couples create this zone of privacy easily and readily. But others get bogged down because one or both finds it difficult to separate out being a couple from being a family. Sometimes a parent is hit hard by the intensity of love felt by and for the child—nothing else seems to come close. The spouse ends up feeling like a third wheel.

If you start viewing each other as nothing more than co-parents, your marriage may hit a dead end when your parenting services are no longer needed. Do your job right and one day your children will up and leave. That day may seem very far away, but time zips along at a disturbingly fast clip once you become a parent. Before you know it a two-wheeler replaces that tricycle. No sooner have the training wheels come off then suddenly you're negotiating driving privileges with a high schooler. And then you're out of a job. That's both cause for celebration and some sorrow. Which of those emotions predominates depends a great deal on whether when you look over at your spouse you see a stranger or the familiar features of a best friend. It's tragic when a couple keeps putting their relationship on hold for the sake of the children. When they finally get around to each other again they find there's no one there.

To make matters worse, spending all of those years back-burnering their relationship has taken a toll on the kids, too. When parents ignore or disrespect their own marriage the child is left with the sense that he is somehow more central to his parent's life than he ought to be. He feels guilty, pressured, suffocated, resentful, or has had to so thoroughly suppress his own needs so his parents can live through him vicariously that he hasn't a clue as to who he is or what he wants out of life.

Often, couples start down this slippery slope by taking their marriage for granted. When your children, spouse and job cry out for undivided attention at the same time the easiest response is to drop the ball with your spouse's name on it. After all, your mate is on your side and will therefore be understanding about your unavailability in a way that a boss, customer or two-year-old will not be. The problem with this approach is that, to keep the juggling metaphor going, these three balls are not of equal weight and size. Your work and children are important, but your marriage is the heaviest, biggest and most weighty of all.

If you're having difficulty enforcing a zone of privacy for your marriage, sometimes all that's really necessary is to realize what has happened and to reach out for your spouse again. Spend time alone together. You needn't always forego "quality time" with your kids in favor of romantic nights out. But you don't do the opposite—you don't neglect or take for granted the deep bond you've forged with your mate. You don't drop the big one.

Stand United

You probably realized the first time you tried to buy a couch together that you don't see eye to eye on everything. So it should come as no surprise that you don't have identical views on how to raise children. Differences are likely to erupt over the countless minutiae of life with child—as well as over relatively important matters such as whether or which kind of religious upbringing to offer. In almost all cases it's in the best interest of your child that you work it out and present a united front.

Being a young child is confusing enough without having to deal with mixed messages. Is it okay to play with the computer mouse? Mommy says, "No!" but when just Dad's around I get to click away. Multiply and magnify this difference and you can see why it causes difficulty for the child. He's trying to understand the world, but the two people he relies on the most keep giving him conflicting information. The result is the child doesn't develop as secure a base. If his parents argue in front of him over their differences without resolving them, further damage is done. On some level he understands that he is at the root of his parents' anger at each other. This is a greater burden than any child should have to bear.

As children get older they become shockingly savvy about deducing the differences of opinion between their parents. They learn to play one off of the other ("But Daddy said I could") and develop the annoying ability to anticipate each parent's response and only ask permission to go mall-hopping from the one who's more likely to assent. So you might as well gain extensive practice in standing united now. Here's how:

Be Upfront.

If you find you've inadvertently contradicted each other in junior's presence, let him listen as you resolve the difference. For example:

Dad: Want another cupcake, pal?
Mom: Er, uh, actually Hon, I just told Roy he'll have to wait till after dinner.
Dad: Okay. Sorry Pal.
Roy: But I want one!
Dad: Mommy's right.

Negotiate In Their Presence.

In instances when your child doesn't feel like you're about to make the most important decision of his or her life (such as whether he can watch Nickelodeon) it can only benefit him to see you negotiate over a difference of opinion. It's okay for him to know that Mom absolutely does not believe in watching TV during dinner but that Dad thinks an exception should be made for the play-offs. As long as you keep it civil, airing your difference in your child's presence can benefit him. It teaches him the important lesson that it's okay to disagree with someone you love and that differences of opinion can be resolved without one person losing and the other winning. The key is to make sure you *do* resolve the issue. Research has shown that the truly toxic part of parental arguments for children occurs when children don't see them making up, resolving their difference in a way they both feel okay about.

All of this takes some soul-searching and foresight on your part. If you don't think you can discuss your disagreement relatively amicably (without calling each other names or being otherwise contemptuous and disrespectful) you absolutely should not try to settle a disagreement concerning your child in front of him.

Keep It in Perspective.

You're upset that your spouse has just agreed to take the kids out for Happy Meals or allowed them to watch a videotape without them first picking up all of the alphabet blocks they've scattered on the floor. Remember that they will suffer far more if you make a scene over it than if you let it go.

Talk about It Later.

Your daughter throws her daddy's slipper down the stairs and he immediately points her in the direction of the time-out chair. You think it would be more effective to make her pick up the slipper and return it to him with an apology. You may be right, but now is not the time to voice your opinion. The rule about creating a united front is a critical one when it comes to discipline. Never undermine each other. Stand united now. Later you can privately discuss your objections and come up with a flying-footwear policy for the future.

But Don't Be Clones

None of this means that parents should be interchangeable. If your parenting differences are more style than substance try not to stifle each other. From your child's early infancy, your differences in approach will be obvious. Nobody rocks, burps or diapers a baby exactly the same way. Some people are very nurturing and cuddly with little ones, others are more playful. That's just fine with baby, who learns that there is more than one acceptable way to be fed, comforted or played with. If you grouse to your spouse because he shampoos junior at the beginning rather than the end of his bath, or burps her on his knee rather than his shoulder, lay off. Everybody benefits when parents allow each other to be themselves.

Likewise, nobody benefits when one parent (and let's face it, it's usually the mom) comes on as the Expert. When one parent insists there's only one way to do things for her child the other one usually backs off, whether out of anger, intimidation, or a desire to keep the peace. The sad result is that the retreating parent may not develop as deep a connection with the child, or confidence in his own ability. Instead of two parents the child ends up with 1 1/2—or one and a clone.

Respect and acknowledge your differences and, as your kids get older, they'll be enriched by your great qualities and buffeted from being harmed by each of your flaws. They'll come to know that Dad is playful, Mom is earnest. They'll understand that Dad tends to have a short fuse over minor things, so it's best to turn to Mom if they break a plate. But when it comes to homework, Dad's the patient one. Most importantly, when they see you accepting and supporting each other despite any differences in taste, style, temperament or astrological sign, they'll realize that there are any number of ways for a person to be, and still be beloved.

Let Them Play Favorites

There will be times when your child will view your spouse as nothing less than an emissary from Mount Olympus while he grants you the same degree of awe he usually reserves for lentils. You sidle into your booth at a diner and your offspring suddenly announces she wants to sit next to Daddy, not you. Or, it's three A.M. and your shrieking, thirsty two-year-old will not accept any water palmed off by her father. "I want Mommy to do it!" is the constant wail. Your spouse walks in the door and all activity ceases, replaced by exultation and celebration. "Daddy's home! Daddy's home!" the kids chant, jumping up and down. When *you* come home your firstborn does not consider the event worthy of removing his focus from his hangnail.

It's a fact of parenthood that kids play favorites. Problems arise if the parents see the child's fickleness as a playing field on which to compete against each other. Vying to be number one in Junior's heart by overtly or subtly encouraging him to love you more can be destructive to your marriage and your child. So remember the rule about maintaining a united front. Don't play favorites with your children, and when they play favorites with you don't egg them on.

Sometimes a child's favoritism is subtle, sometimes the hostility toward one parent is so thick it's troubling. No one can give you a quickie diagnosis for why your particular child has placed you or your spouse in the dog house of late or whether it is reason for concern. But all else being standard issue about your child—meaning developmentally and physically everything seems to be going relatively fine—and the snubbing hasn't gone on for months or years, it's probably nothing to worry about. It's simply part of growing up. At different stages of a child's life he gravitates toward one parent or the other for any number of reasons. Sometimes it's that one parent's personality is more in synch with the child's right now. Or, a child trying to understand gender may hover around the parent of that gender (or the other). Sometimes the lopsided affection is as simple as having missed one parent more than the other of late.

No treatise on this subject, however brief, would be complete without a mention of King Oedipus, in honor of whom Sigmund Freud named that complex which remains a linchpin of psychoanalytic theory. Whatever you think of Freudian analysis, don't be shocked if you note a shade of romantic longing for you from your child of the opposite sex (though there's no need to worry if you don't). The five-year-old boy says his mommy is so very cozy as he settles in for a cuddle. The four-year-old girl in her bridal costume announces her plan to marry Daddy. Make of it what you will, but it's there. The best thing you can do when your daughter bats her lashes at her dad and treats you like the evil stepmother (or vice versa) is to have a sense of humor. Accept it for what it is—a normal stage that will pass. Don't tease your child, but don't take her snubbing (or adulation) seriously. To the degree you can indulge her preference without infringing on other's rights or inconveniences, do so. No, Mommy shouldn't have to get the cup of juice if Daddy is already awake and ready to pour. But there's no harm in granting a child's request to sit next to her current favorite at the diner or to have Mommy rather than Daddy read her a goodnight story.

But it's also important to guide your child toward seeing that playing favorites can be hurtful. By three or four, children do come to understand that their words and actions can affect other people. But it's still almost implausible to them that they could truly wound one of their all-powerful parents. No harm, and a lot of good, can come if you point out to the child that saying he doesn't like you or never wants to sit next to you makes you sad. But avoid being heavy-handed about it. Playing favorites is standard behavior for this age so you don't want to try to instill guilt in your child for doing what comes naturally.

If your child really does seem to be infatuated with one parent or the other the best approach is to be understanding about the child's longings, but also make it clear who's who and what's what. Usually, when Ethan's Daddy announced a business trip Ethan would whine that he didn't want Daddy to go. But at four that whining was replaced by a look of calculation in his young eyes. "Good," he announced matter-of-factly. "I can sleep in your bed with Mommy." Obviously, Ethan needed to be told gently that his parents' bed was not his place, whether his dad was at home or in Ukraine. Ethan wasn't happy to hear the news, but life is filled with such necessary disappointments.

Even if their spouse isn't encouraging the favoritism, some parents take it to heart when their child shows a preference for the other. The pain can go pretty deep when your child rebuffs you—especially if you're feeling lousy about yourself for any other reasons. Repeat to yourself over and over that your child's feelings are perfectly normal and not any indication of your real worth to him or the world. You wouldn't take as gospel a two-year-old's assessment of anything else, so why should his current view of your parenting skills merit serious consideration? Expect to spend plenty of time on and off his top-ten list. Also expect that once adolescent hormones begin to surge both of you may be removed from it for extended periods. Just pray you live long enough for your child to rediscover how adorable you are after all.

Let Them See You Make Up

There was a time when experts believed the longevity and happiness quotient of the typical marriage depended in good part on whether the couple fought a lot. Due to Dr. John Gottman's pioneering work at the University of Seattle in Washington, we now know that what makes or breaks a marriage is a lot more complicated than the frequency and intensity of your spats. In fact, whether a couple fights a lot or not at all may not point to the state of their union as much as its *style*. Some couples are always polite with each other, meanwhile their neighbors readily engage in verbal brawls over whether to buy tuna packed in oil or in water. Neither or both couples may be headed for divorce—their style of conflict is not telltale.

But one thing research shows clearly no matter how you and your spouse address conflicts: Marital tension can be very damaging to children. Kids raised in homes where the marriage is a misery display all the signs of deep emotional distress—from difficulty with peers to problems at school to increased mental illness.

If your marriage is in trouble it's obviously best for your entire family if you seek responsible, professional help. But what if your marriage is not teetering on dissolution, yet still has its rough patches or days? How can you best protect your children when they've seen and heard you angry with each other—or are feeling unsettled by a silence between you that speak volumes, even to a five-year-old?

For children, one of the most damaging aspects of witnessing marital tension—whether it's an argument during a car trip or the angry slamming of a door—is that they often don't get to witness its ending. In an effort to spare their children, parents try to keep their conflicts to themselves. So when one erupts they may finish it in private to protect the child from hearing their angry words and voices. Although this approach is understandable, it robs the child of the opportunity to see you resolve the problem and make up. As upsetting as marital spats can be to children, they create less anxiety if you let your kids see that the world (and your marriage) isn't coming to an end. Since they know you're arguing, let them witness you talking it out and then getting over it. Seeing you happy together again teaches them that it is possible to disagree with someone you love—even get angry at him or her—and still live happily ever after.

Chapter Nine

THE ULTIMATE RULE

Know When to Break the Rules

In the months and years ahead there will be times when, thanks to your growing store of wisdom, you will see that sometimes the Rules don't apply. Every child and every situation is different. Sometimes there is no good choice as a parent, just a choice that isn't as bad as the others. So, in certain situations, you may decide that it's best to threaten a child with no dessert or to give him a clear sense of how very impatient you are feeling.

But even when you go against a Rule, try not to waver from the fundamental conviction on which all of the Rules are based: respect for your child. If you're unsure whether to break with principle in a particular situation ask yourself: Is this in the best interest of my child? Am I showing proper regard for my child's desires as well as for his or her needs? Can I live with this decision tomorrow? Soul-searching in this way will help you steer clear of being overly permissive or rigid with kids. Children need our guidance— sometimes very firm guidance. But you can't effectively offer it unless you remember that even the littlest among us deserve respect. Sometimes rules are made to be broken. But a child's spirit should never be.